Figuring It Out

And by that, I mean that I still am.

Copyright 2006 NSB

ISBN 978-0-9792163-0-5
ISBN 0-9792163-0-3

For those who know what it feels like to "figure it out," those who have helped them along the way, and especially for those who have done both – because sometimes you can't see what's inside of you until you see it in others.

Figuring It Out

I'm not stupid enough to think that I don't matter. Believing that I don't matter would be a mental suicide. If I believe that, I'll never get to where I want to go, and where I want to go is away. I want to go far away to a place where I can make it on my own and earn respect from others and from myself. The best I can do right now is to imagine what it will be like; what I want it to be like. Because I think that if you've got the vision, the determination, and the plan, it's halfway done.

-Me

May 1, 1997

I was 15 years old.

INTRODUCTION

I was terrified of coming out. I was so terrified that for more than ten years, I told myself that I didn't know if I was gay.

I knew enough that I started hiding things about myself when I was around ten years old. I knew there was something different about the way I wanted to keep rewinding that part of that movie, just so I could see *her* smile again. I knew I couldn't keep talking about this girl at school, because someone would guess that I liked her.

I feel like I knew all of these things before I even knew what being gay was. So maybe I didn't have a label for it, yet. I just knew that I was supposed to like boys, but I liked girls better.

When I started putting this book together, I thought about what I was hoping to accomplish by allowing people such an intimate look into... well... Me. Despite the obvious risk, I felt that there was a need because I hadn't yet seen anything quite like what I had in mind for this project.

As a society, we are getting better at telling stories in the media about the struggles that take place between gay people and the world we live in – coming out stories, the things that happen between children and parents, and the things that gay people have to deal with because they are gay.

We even address what happens within a gay relationship that makes it different from straight relationships – when one person is out, but the other isn't; when they want to get married; adopt or have children; have the same privileges and benefits as heterosexual couples; when decisions must be made in the event of a death, and on and on.

But we don't see much about the internal struggle a person must go through in the process of realizing and accepting themselves as being gay – the inner monologue as it progresses from a subconscious knowledge of a difference, to consciousness and all of the phases that make up the journey to living the truth.

That's what this project was and is – an attempt to expose that inner monologue. I hope that by my doing so, others like me will find a kind of companionship - in knowing that other people have thought the same things, and in knowing that people continue to struggle, because this is an individual's struggle. For me, this was the hardest part because I felt like I was alone.

It can't be avoided until we, as a world, can be accepting and unassuming. I sometimes wonder if being unassuming might be equally as important as acceptance. We can be accepting, but if we keep on acting as though everyone is "straight by default" - if it keeps being that people must *come out* in order to be known, then it's still a struggle; a decision of what and when to say if one figures it out. And it doesn't quite acknowledge the equality of people.

What follows is my coming out story, as told through my writing over a period of 9 years. It begins at Age 15, partly because that's when I started writing about my emotions, rather than the details of my day-to-day life – and partly because everything before that should be saved for my future autobiography. The bulk of it takes place in Ages 22-24 because that's when I was writing every day. Here and there you'll find essays and the occasional one-liner, which are my commentary in hindsight.

I have cut out a lot of driveling crap. But not so much as to de-humanize it. It reads something like therapy. One thing I kept reminding myself was that this had to remain an honest, deeply flawed, often embarrassing in its inexperience, vaguely idiotic expression of life. I think I have succeeded.

AGE 15

Everyone needs
someone to talk to.

April 11, 1997

I've been asking myself more and more lately: What do I want? And I'm in the midst of discovering that the answer is not an easy one and that actually obtaining it will be even harder.

May 2, 1997

I watched an episode of *Ellen* this week – the one where she tells everyone that she's gay. The comedian playing Ellen – Ellen DeGeneres – is also gay. It made me think – what would I do if I realized I was gay? It's not something you can change, or even hide very well.

Just something to think about.

June 3, 1997

Well, we're having another mini-crisis; I can hear the shouting. My parents are so stupid about some things. They're lucky we turned out the way we did. But still, I don't misbehave out of fear of what they might do to me. I don't think that's how it's supposed to be.

June 9, 1997

He called me stupid. He called me dumb. He is the man that I call my father, and I could point out a hundred things about him that I hate – but the one that stands out the most is his impossibly short temper.

They don't understand that what I want is their love and attention.

August 14, 1997

I've been trying to determine what this feeling is that makes me feel like… I don't know, exactly. Fear, anxiety, hope, happiness…? It's a combination of all kinds of things.

I need someone. To talk to, to share with. But I suppose that person is far into the future, if I will have someone like that at all. I hope that someday when I read this, I will have accomplished whatever I'm wishing for now. I hope I find that person.

August 25, 1997

The world is a strange place. Half the time, I'm trying to figure out whether I love it or hate it. The other half, I'm trying to stay alive.

The battles we face every day, the relationships we risk, what is it all for in the end? Will there ever be a time when you can look back and say, "I did that for this reason?" And is it a good reason? Or is it all for nothing?

I'm only 15. That's what makes things hard. But it's also what makes the other things easy. I'm only 15 – yet I'm trying to figure out the world already. To figure out the world, you can't think like an adult. Because they're the ones who screwed it up in the first place. You can't think like a kid, either, because kids... well, they're kids.

I think you have to think from somewhere in between – somewhere that no one would expect any brains to be, because of a stereotype. A simple, stupid stereotype that teenagers are self-centered and greedy, with no conscience – that they need you to come clean their ass because they are incapable of thinking for themselves and following through with the appropriate action.

September 18, 1997

I want to be happy and free. A perfect way to describe it is like in those scenes in movies where the character is driving down the highway, car windows rolled down, radio turned up to a feel-good song. It's sunny, a perfect day, and they're singing along with the radio with their best friend next to them in the passenger seat.

I want to do that – someday, I'll do that. It's just a feeling that I really want to experience – one where all you have to think about is what's happening at that very instant, and nothing else matters. It's a moment that you want to freeze-frame and save, so you can go back to it and recapture that feeling whenever you want.

September 27, 1997

Sometimes I feel so trapped. I want out of here so bad it almost hurts, physically. I wish I could ditch this life and live a better one.

I mean, I have friends… It's just that I don't connect so well with them. I don't connect so well with anybody, it seems. I can't seem to see past everything that's only skin deep – I don't know who they really are, but then I suppose they don't know me all that well, either.

When I get into moods like this one, I end up kind of retreating into myself. I exist only in my head. That's when I'll get all kinds of thoughts and things, and it's hard for me to interact with people. I'll speak when spoken to, smile when I know I should, but otherwise just sit there with a blank expression on my face.

All my feelings seem to be dulled when I'm in that kind of mood. Sometimes it's good, sometimes it sucks. Either way, I don't think I can help it.

October 5, 1997

There are some days when I just start to think about things, and I panic. I wonder what will happen to me in the future – will all of my work be for nothing? Will I achieve none of my dreams? Will I become the one thing that I don't want to be? I don't know, and that's what scares me.

Sometimes the pressures are just too great, and I want to drop everything, sit down, or lie down, close my eyes, and drift away. Off to a place where I don't have to worry about anything. I'd even settle for being transported into my future – at least it'll save me the wondering and anticipation.

I am so lonely. I have friends, but I don't think they'd want to hear this. I have parents, but how am I supposed to talk to them? All my mom does is talk about how I make her life a living hell. My dad demands to know why I make things so damn hard for everyone. I honestly don't know. I don't do these things on purpose. I'm not consciously bad. I don't do things that can fairly be classified as bad.

I read somewhere that kids who misbehave, do so because they know that no matter what, they will be loved. But I don't misbehave because I'm scared to death of what might happen if I did. Would they disown me? Cut off all my privileges? Dismiss me totally and completely? I don't know. But I don't feel very loved.

I have no one to talk to or touch me lovingly. Sometimes, it hurts. And other times, I'm glad, because I believe that it's making me a stronger person.

October 13, 1997

Before, I thought that good writing was something that other people would like when they read it. But I realize now that good writing is honest writing. You just have to write what you feel.

October 29, 1997

Every time my parents have a big fight, I think - will this be the argument that forces them to take that much-anticipated leap -

divorce? Sometimes I think it would be better for them and us, to just do it already. No more daily fights, frequent violent outbursts that inevitably end with my father leaving the house.

It terrifies me to see his face, creased with stress and anger, and his voice high and strained. Then I'll hear a crash or a boom and I'll know that he has either hit something or knocked something over.

I'm afraid that if something isn't done soon, my mother and sisters will be scarred for life, not physically, but emotionally and psychologically. I'm not worried about myself – I know that I could just pick up and move on; I'm in touch with my own feelings enough to stay sane.

November 2, 1997

I hope that someday I'll know what it feels like to be loved – truly loved. I never understood why girls want boyfriends so much; only now am I beginning to understand.

I want someone to share things with. What would it be like to talk to someone who felt the same way I do about things – someone who wouldn't laugh at me (except at my jokes, of course). Someone who wanted the same things I did; someone who understands.

Maybe I'm asking too much. That's what I'm afraid of. What if there is no such person? I don't know. I believe it could happen. I think that I need to believe it could happen.

November 11, 1997

Why do I feel like my life is so empty? It's not physically empty; I do things every day. It's emotionally empty. I have nothing to believe in except myself. No one to hang on to, no reassurance to keep me going.

There's a big hole right in the middle of everything, and it's throwing me off. I want something to fill that empty space. I need it. I need someone to love me, I need to believe that they love me, I need to love them, and I need for them to believe that I love them.

November 18, 1997

When the world around me closes in, I retreat to the only haven that I know. It's a place I can visit no matter where I am, and when I step over the threshold, I'm overwhelmed by the vast expanse of something that I shouldn't even try to explain.

It's ironic that retreating into my head, into my own thoughts, gives me such a sense of freedom. It's the only place where I can honestly express anything and everything without being judged. And others wonder why I love this place so much.

To be shy and almost reclusive is looked down upon, in society. People are encouraged to go out and party, meet others; socialize.

I think I'm waiting to find that person who will restore my faith in humankind. That someone will love me just as much as I love them, and won't be afraid to show it.

People can be so mean sometimes. But they can also be the greatest things in the world. I'm trying to remember that.

November 26, 1997

Unconditional love. I hope that before I die, I get to experience love without limits, without boundaries. I don't have that right now. Or at least it doesn't feel like it. You know you don't have unconditional love when you're always afraid of losing peoples' favor, of screwing up so they don't like you anymore. But it exists; I'm sure of that. And I'm going to find it.

December 14, 1997

Homesickness. That's what it is. I'm homesick for a place I've never been, for feelings I've never felt. I've been asking myself: What exactly is love, and what do I need out of it? The answer isn't easy. I'm still working on it.

December 18, 1997

I wish I were someone else. But then I realize: If I were someone else, I wouldn't be me. I like who I am. I want to see what I can do with myself, how far I can go. I see it as a challenge that is meant to be achieved. Who knows if I actually will, right?

It's just so damn frustrating, especially at this time of year. Christmas. I realize that even if I'm not happy, I should try to pretend to be, because why ruin the spirit for everyone else?

But then I wonder, what exactly is the Christmas spirit? Shouldn't Christmas involve just people getting along? It should involve utter happiness for all. Twenty-four hours in which there is not a worry in the world, and everyone is completely happy for once. That's all I want. I'll forgo the presents. I want someone to make me laugh and smile; I want to make someone laugh and smile.

February 4, 1998

You know, my father has one of the shortest tempers ever. It doesn't take the drop of a pin before he starts raising his voice, and pretty soon it's full-on ranting and raving. He gets really mad, and it scares me.

I used to get mad, too, when he got mad at me. I used to cry after he yelled at me. But I've gotten used to it. Now, my feelings sort of shut down. When he starts to turn his anger on me, I force myself to feel flat. Don't react, don't let it bother me because it's just another episode.

I wish he could see himself through my eyes. I don't bother wasting feelings on him anymore. But sometimes, he still scares me.

March 14, 1998

There are never any real answers, are there? I mean like answers to universal questions – Why isn't the world fair? Why are people bad? Why are people good? When will it end? Will it ever end?

It's useless to ponder these questions, because all you realize is that there are no answers.

I hope I never ever lose sight of myself. I hope that I never become something just because other people want me to. And I hope that I never let people force me into not being who I really am, just because it's weird.

AGE 16

Life is hard.
I think that's the extent
of the proverbial secret.
Life is just hard.

April 15, 1998

Sometimes I wish my friends knew about my problems at home, because maybe then they'd understand me a little more; believe that some things I say are not exaggerations.

And then I think, why should they have to know? I should be strong enough to do things on my own. I want to be that strong. But it's so lonely, and yet, instead of reaching out to people, I feel like I'm pushing them away. Even though they're the ones I want approval from, I push them away.

Maybe I was always like this – pushing people away. And even if I want to be intimate with somebody, maybe I just can't. Maybe I won't let myself do it, no matter how much I want to. How devastating that would be.

April 23, 1998

There are so many things that I'm pissed about. It might be irrational, but still. These things really bother me. But I try not to let certain things show. I want to find someone to truly trust with all my being.

May 2, 1998

I fear that with every passing day, I'm becoming more and more narrow-minded. I don't know if this is really happening, or if it's all in my head. But the last thing I want to do is become narrow-minded. It's one of my greatest fears.

I suppose I have some control over it. But it's hard to maintain that openness when everyone around me is narrow-minded. It just irritates me. I wish I had someone to talk to – someone who I wouldn't mind telling my every thought to.

November 23, 1998

I just thought that I should write down a few things – a few facts, just for the record.

My father just called me a bitch. Let's add that to the list. Let's see… there was "stupid," I think that was the first one, and then there was "idiot"… then of course sometimes he brings out the "what the hell is wrong with you" argument.

My mother doesn't do anything about it, though. She just sits by and never does a thing to lessen it or stop it. I think she's afraid of him. I know I am.

December 17, 1998

Intangible forces confuse me. Fate. Spirits of the dead. Psychic powers. Vibes. The way you can just feel some things without ever really knowing them.

Are there such things? Or are we looking for something to believe in, to soften the blow of reality? Sometimes I think that I believe. But at other times, I wonder how it could be true – how such things could possibly exist, within the world that we know, so dominated by science which rules out these occurrences as coincidences, or even worse, as figments of the imagination.

And I realize that I do want to believe. I want to believe in a world where we will never be alone. And fate – resigning yourself over to what a higher power says is meant for you? Somewhat relieving.

March 10, 1999

So… what? I'm confused right now, and what's frustrating is that I don't even know what I'm confused about, so I can't even write about it. I suffer from major moments of feeling inadequate and major bouts of jealousy. …I just have to find a way to stop feeling like this.

DANA
Have you ever not wanted to go home?

JOE
Well, I guess everybody wishes they could just pick up and go away for awhile.

DANA
No, I mean – have you ever felt like you were signing your own death sentence by going home every night? Like you don't know how long you can keep blocking out all the bad stuff and still be okay. And you're just afraid.

AGE 17

I wish
I had the courage
to not care
what others think of me.

May 15, 1999

What is it about human nature that enables us to be so utterly and completely confused? Why are we plagued by such things as emotions, and why do we have the means to abuse these emotions so?

May 22, 1999

I think that my greatest battle will be to allow myself to be and feel loved. In accepting love, I will be able to love. I can't only give love and not be receptive to it, or take love and not be as giving – it's impossible; it doesn't work that way. It's a both-or-nothing deal.

I'm having a hard time grasping this thing they call "reality." And reality, with such harsh connotations is really overwhelming and intimidating. How are you supposed to believe in fairy tales and wishes coming true – in short, be optimistic? I know that I used to be. And I know that somehow, I've become hardened and cynical – pessimistic. I'd like the old innocence back, but I suppose it left with childhood.

May 30, 1999

The mysteries of the heart are as elusive as the mysteries of the universe, perhaps even more so. For although each of us may hold the answers to the questions of human nature, few ever fully gasp their meaning. Conversely, the vastness of the universe suggests that its answers are meant to remain out of reach, yet we have accomplished, discovered, transcended… beyond reasonable expectation.

What insists that we must look beyond our world, putting science before feeling, while the enigma of the human heart remains unsolved? In the world as it is today, men of science outnumber poets, society holds doctors in higher esteem than aspiring authors who seek to expose the secrets of human nature, and very few people will sit still for the most brilliantly made, insightful, true-to-life character piece, while everyone will flock to see the latest action-adventure, blood-and-guts, science-fiction thriller.

This is not to denounce all sciences, of course. The difference in values and character from generation to generation, then, is perhaps the fault of society, that factual knowledge and the scientific process take precedent over the hows and whys of natural impulse and the most forgotten treasure of human existence: instinct.

August 17, 1999

I feel so much, and yet most of it can't be put into words – it's meant just to be felt, I guess. Or to be expressed physically, when the right time comes. It's all this waiting that really gets to people, I think. Waiting for whatever the world will do so that the pieces just click and they find eternal bliss, or happiness ever after, or some overrated trick or other. I'm waiting, too.

AGE 18

Maybe this
will make me stronger
for real life.

'You bring out the worst in people.
It's your fault.'

            'You're a fucking pain in the ass,
                        that's what you are.'

'I don't know how somebody who's supposedly so smart
can be so stupid.'

            'You deserve to be sworn at.'

'Sometimes I just want to punch you in the face.'

Click.

The lock fell into place, and she backed up against the wall and slid to the bathroom floor. For a second, the thought entered her mind that he might be crazed and angry enough to find a screwdriver and take the lock off the door.

She looked up at the window in the wall to her right. The narrow opening was about a foot and a half wide, by three feet tall. She could probably push out the screen if she really wanted to. It was rainy and cold outside, but she'd do it if he tried to get to her.

She envisioned herself climbing up and squeezing out the window, only to land barefoot in the wet grass of the backyard.

What would she do, then? There was nowhere to hide outside. She was better off in here – drier and warmer, though she was beginning to feel a chill from sitting on the blue-gray tiles.

She was glad that the bathroom was small – a half-bath with only a sink and a toilet. The walls hugged her. She could feel the enclosed space, and it was safe. Nothing in here was going to touch her.

Somewhere else in the house, a door slammed, causing the one in front of her to vibrate and shake in its frame. Her eyes flew to the knob. Still locked.

She didn't cry. There was a difference between crying and shedding tears, and she didn't cry. It wasn't a matter of pride; it was a matter of principle. He had made her cry too many times, for too stupid and insignificant reasons. He had no right, and she wouldn't have it anymore. She was stronger than him.

So maybe it was a matter of pride, after all.

She told herself that she was better than that. If it was really true, or if it was one of those lies that one tells oneself in order to survive, she wouldn't venture to guess. But she knew that if it had started out as a lie, it wouldn't be on the day she died. He'd said things to her that she vowed never to say to her own children. If she ever had any.

(In Hindsight)

GLASS HALF-EMPTY...
OR IS IT TWO GLASSES, HALF-FULL?

One morning, at breakfast – I must have been in high school at the time – I had a drink of orange juice. I'm not a big juice-drinker, so it was rare that I did this.

Then I wanted some water, but as everyone knows, water isn't as good if it tastes faintly of orange juice – so I took a clean plastic cup and drank from that.

My father came into the kitchen, and when he saw what I had done, he was furious. At the time, he was responsible for washing most of the dishes, so within twenty seconds, he was yelling in anger at the fact that I had just dirtied two cups at one meal.

I was not aware of any signs that should have cautioned me that frivolous dish-usage was grounds for a verbal beating.

I stood there, not saying anything. I had not said anything since admitting responsibility for the two cups.

I silently witnessed the escalation of his anger. It was as if he was feeding on his own negative energy. It was bizarre in a way that momentarily took me out of myself and allowed me to hover nearby, observing.

I don't remember how it ended; if I waited for him to stop yelling, or if I walked away in the middle of it, or even if I washed the two dirty cups.

I do remember that I had a moment of clarity as I watched myself standing there. He yelled all the time, but that was the first time I was absolutely certain that I had not deserved any of what he obviously thought I did.

I think I had it worse than my sisters because I was the only one who ever fought back. I couldn't bear not to, and now I realize that the reason why I fought so hard was because I wanted so badly to convince him that I was worthy of his approval, even if I had my own thoughts and feelings.

It was a choice I didn't want to make – have a self, or have his love.

The choice was simpler when I no longer wanted both.

I'm grateful that I valued myself enough to fight. In that sense, I don't think I can ever lose or neglect who I am to me.

To let myself be known to others is a greater challenge, especially if I feel like I have something to lose. But sometimes it seems that one's most passionate desires are fulfilled only if life is lived as though one has everything to lose and nothing to lose at the same time.

I am worthy, I think. It just takes guts. And to find that thing you want more than anything else in the universe.

AGE 19

What I wouldn't give to
know what we're all
searching for.

INT. WINNEBAGO - DAY

          JENNY
Truth.

          RYAN
Okay - greatest injustice.

          JENNY
To me?

          RYAN
To you, witnessed, committed, whatever.

          JENNY
Any instance where someone is hurt because of the way they were born is the greatest injustice.

          RYAN
Such as?

          JENNY
I don't know; discrimination on the basis of race; genocide. You can take it on that scale, or it could be as simple and

>   everyday as someone not
>   getting a job because
>   they're in a
>   wheelchair. Prejudice,
>   you know?
>
>   RYAN
>   That's just - life.
>   That's practically
>   everything about life.
>
>   JENNY
>   And we don't care, do
>   we? Until it happens
>   to us.
>
> Ryan shrugs.
>
>   JENNY
>   I used to think... I
>   might be gay.
>
>   RYAN
>   I   thought   that,   too…
>   About you.
>
>   JENNY
>   Don't be an ass - I was
>   terrified to think I
>   might be a lesbian.
>   There's the injustice.
>   That fear.

You said you wanted to fly away,
And you asked me:
If you could fly away,
Where would you go?

And I just stared.

And you said,
If I could fly away,
I'd go everywhere
There was no pain.
Everywhere there was no anger.
Everywhere there was no sadness.

You said,

If I could fly away,
I'd go everywhere
Where nobody fought.

And then you stopped me from speaking,
And said:
Well, then, I'd go everywhere
There were no people.

And there was silence
As you thought some more;
As I thought what to say.

And you said,
If I could fly away,
I'd go somewhere
Where I couldn't remember.
Somewhere so this didn't exist.
Somewhere I could start over.

You said,
If I could fly away,
I'd go somewhere
Where I could forget.

And then you stopped me from speaking,
And said:
I don't need those memories.

And you asked me again:
If you could fly away,
Where would you go?

And I was afraid to answer,
Because it had to be perfect.

So I thought,
And finally said:
If I could fly away,
I'd follow you.

And you smiled and shook your head,
And I knew it was okay,
Even though you knew that
If I could fly away,
I wouldn't.

The "you" and the "I" in the poem are both me. Trying to convince myself to stay.

AGE 20

Sometimes I wonder
if I'll ever be
enough for myself.

INT. SARAH'S APARTMENT - NIGHT

Sarah sits on the couch while Haley paces.

> HALEY
> I don't know what the hell this means. I always told myself that I liked watching actresses more because I looked up to them. I told myself that I saw them as role models, and I wanted to be like them. That I identified with them. But I can't keep denying -

> SARAH
> Hey - relax.

> HALEY
> Don't tell me to relax. You know what this is like.

> SARAH
> Slow down.

Haley keeps pacing, speaking distractedly.

                    HALEY
          Okay. Okay. Slow
          down. People go
          through phases, right?
          I just...

                    SARAH
          You can't be sure until
          you've tried it. It's
          okay.

                    HALEY
          I don't want to use
          you.

                    SARAH
          Would you be?

Haley doesn't answer.

                    SARAH
          Scary as shit, isn't
          it?

Sarah moves to stand in front of
Haley.

                    SARAH
          Well, I want this.

She kisses Haley softly - an
innocent kiss that barely lasts a
few seconds. As they slowly pull

apart, Haley stares, frozen.

Sarah turns to go back to the couch, but Haley catches her arm.

This kiss is heated, desperate, and much more involved than the last. Long moments pass before they come up for air.

Haley shakes her head.

> SARAH
> What?

> HALEY
> I feel like -

> SARAH
> What?

> HALEY
> Like I'm dying and being reborn at the same time.

> SARAH
> That's how it's supposed to feel.

October 6, 2002

I'm getting a little wary of some of my recent physical ailments. I'm suspicious that they might be psychosomatic. I have a sore throat that came on last night after I wrote a scene involving a lesbian kiss. I think I'm afraid that it means I'm gay. But writing something like that doesn't necessarily mean that I am what I write.

I have had questions about my sexuality before. But I don't think I've had enough experience heterosexually to decide if it is or isn't for me... Then again, maybe that's just an excuse I give because I don't want to admit to the truth. I think I need to make out with a boy or two.

October 14, 2002

In movies or TV shows or stories, when a character is troubled, they go off by themselves somewhere and sit in the dark. No matter where they go, or what time of night it is, someone comes along to be the "shoulder to cry on," the "words of wisdom," the "listening ear." The character is then saved, feels so much better, and a new and stronger bond has formed between the two that reinforces or changes their relationship for the better.

This never happens in real life. In real life, everyone else wants their sleep, so they're not going to come and find you at 2:13 in the morning. And if they did, they'd probably walk right past you to the bathroom or to the refrigerator, do what they came to do, and walk right past you again, back to bed.

I wish it worked like it did in the movies. I wish someone would come after me. I guess no one knows me quite that well, and I always wonder if maybe that's my own fault.

HALEY
You were right. I am hiding. I try to tell myself that maybe my feelings mean one thing, but it's only because I don't want to admit what they really mean. And I can't just - I can't just be okay with it. I was thinking the other day... How wonderful would it be if I could watch a movie and not worry if my face betrayed the fact that I had more interest in the female characters than in the male characters? Or what it would be like to feel comfortable admitting that I found a woman sexy. Or how it would be the greatest thing in the world to let myself feel romantic love for someone without needing to hide it to be accepted. You know? And I want all of that.

And I know that the issues are bigger than just me, and that the world is bigger than just me, but me is all I have control over. People say that hiding is easy, but it's not. It's just as tough as being honest. So why not be happy?

AGE 21

Unrequited love.
It's a horrible, horrible thing
to be on the giving end of.
Because you're not receiving.
And I don't mean
for this to sound selfish,
but that really is
the bad part about it.

sometime in 2003 (actual date unknown)

Social anxiety, social phobia, whatever it is – self-diagnosed. Maybe it is a self-fulfilling prophecy, but that's one of its characteristics. I'm a textbook case. A light textbook case, but textbook nonetheless. Sometimes it's worse than others, but being scrutinized is always a trauma. Writing words that I sometimes don't let come. And the pen gets cut off like so many feelings that go unrealized to the world, and I think nobody knows, but maybe they already do and are just waiting for me to say something so they can say, "We knew it the whole time," and having had all that time, are more okay with it than I am so that the only thing I have to adjust to is how cool everyone is about it.

I fell in love for the first time.

With a straight girl, of course.

Except for a string of visits to a few different doctors, none of whom could find anything wrong with me that couldn't be cured with some antidepressants, it was like nothing had ever happened.

Nothing had.

But that's when I started writing every day. Lucky for you.

(In Hindsight)

IF GAYNESS PERSISTS OR WORSENS, CONTACT YOUR PHYSICIAN IMMEDIATELY.

I couldn't eat, I didn't want to sleep, and I felt like a hammer was pounding in my chest. So I did what any other person in love would do – I went to the doctor and told her that something was wrong with my heart.

I didn't know I was being metaphorical; I thought I might be dying.

"Palpitations," I told the doctor, "And a kind of pressure in my chest. ...I already have a heart murmur."

It was true; I did already have a heart murmur, diagnosed years ago by my pediatrician. All it means is that one of my heart valves collapses early, so that instead of "ba-boom, ba-boom," my heartbeat goes "ba-da-boom, ba-da-boom."

It's not very serious, except that no dentist will as much as tell me to open unless I have chugged half a bottle of antibiotics. Something about plaque getting into the bloodstream. I guess that could be fatal for some people.

In any case, my doctor was wise and sent me in to have an ultrasound done on my heart and an x-ray taken of my chest. The ultrasound confirmed the heart murmur but nothing else, and the x-ray was forwarded to a specialist for a second opinion. (The first being my doctor's, that it looked "a little weird.") I took a blood test, too, which I must have passed.

For the heart murmur, the doctor prescribed atenolol, which is something that old people take for high blood pressure.

In the meantime, the presumptive diagnosis for my overall problem was gastro esophageal reflux disease. It is exactly what it sounds like – heartburn from hell. I knew the diagnosis was wrong because it would have involved cutting back on fried foods and watching what I ate, and I just knew that I wasn't going to have that kind of a disease. Out of spite, I went to Burger King for lunch. And then I took the acid reflux medication, anyway.

I kept a food diary for about a week, until I got too pissed off. My last entry read, "I ate a cow." I'm sure I didn't, really.

The second opinion came back, and I was sent for a CT scan of my chest because they suspected that I might still have an organ that normally evolves out of the body once a person grows out of childhood. I didn't really know what to do with that, except to wait.

The CT scan declared me perfectly healthy and devoid of any prepubescent organs. It did locate a cyst on my liver which the doctor said was probably benign. And then she sent me for an ultrasound on my liver – which also revealed me to be perfectly healthy.

The presumptive diagnosis became anxiety induced by stress. I decided that there was probably some truth to that. The doctor prescribed me some Paxil and referred me to the in-house therapist. I never got around to seeing the therapist, but I sure did take the Paxil.

I tried it out for three weeks, during which I was zombie-ish; sleepy all the time as if I were living in a daze or fog, but at the same time – sleepless; less talkative, with a nervous twitch in my leg, and suspiciously not horny. All unfortunate side-effects. Even the lack of a sex drive, given that I had just started dating my now-ex-boyfriend - who, incidentally, was not who I was in love with. (We all do things that we don't want to explain.)

I went back to the doctor and told her that I didn't like Paxil. We decided to start weaning me from it. I thought this was a good idea, so I started taking down the dose. The plan was to reduce it by half, every week or so.

Then one night, at around 11 p.m., I had an episode of impaired vision. It felt like my eyeballs were moving back and forth very quickly; I couldn't focus. By 1 a.m., my ear hurt, I was dizzy, and I had a headache. It was at its worst around 5 a.m., but was better by 8 a.m., except for the headache which faded soon after.

I was a bit freaked out, so I called one of my friends whose father is a doctor, and he said that I was experiencing symptoms of Paxil withdrawal. What a relief that that's what it was. I thought.

The relief came from the fact that I had suspected that my symptoms were the result of a reaction between a Caribbean Rum Ball that I ate, and the drugs I was on. For people who don't know, a Caribbean Rum Ball is a piece of candy that is basically sugar and rum. I had two. Talk about lack of judgment. Although none of the drugs I was on said not to have alcohol (they just said not to have *a lot* of alcohol), there are many more intelligent things to do than to take a few pills and chase them with rum balls. Like not to.

The relief was short-lived, though, because it got worse. When you see movies about drug addicts going through withdrawal – Paxil withdrawal involves all of those symptoms, but on a smaller scale. So I wasn't puking my guts out, but I did spend some time staring into the toilet bowl. Waking up soaked in sweat, dizzy, twitching sensations in my extremities, feeling like I couldn't get out of bed. And it comes in waves.

Not what you'd expect from a medication designed to treat anxiety.

I had been on the full dose for only three weeks. I called my doctor and she put me back on it.

We tried again, taking down the dose slower, this time. I became an expert at cutting pills. I almost felt like a real addict. I got down to one fourth of a pill, every three days. Then I tried stopping again.

When that didn't work, I got scared. I couldn't cut the pills smaller than one fourth, and three days was about the longest I could go between doses without experiencing any serious symptoms. My doctor was at a loss, as well.

While all of this was happening, I had done some research on Paxil (good idea) and found that my problem was widespread. Thousands of people were having problems stopping this drug – it was tougher than anyone had anticipated; doctors included. Its short half-life made it one of the most difficult prescription drugs to quit.

My third attempt to stop failed, so I concentrated on stabilizing myself at the smallest dose possible, which was still a fourth of a pill every three days. In the midst of that, I learned that the specific kind of Paxil I was taking was no longer being manufactured. I didn't waste time thinking about the implications of their decision to discontinue this medication. I had roughly 30 pills left, which theoretically would have lasted me almost a year, but by that time I'd been on Paxil for six months. A year didn't seem like a very long time. And those pills were hard to cut. I had to assume that a good portion of them would not be usable.

I decided that I was going to have to seek treatment as if I were a real live drug addict. I went on the internet and found an Addiction Psychiatrist. I refused to believe that someone who had helped heroin addicts would not be able to help me. At least my drug was legal.

So I went to this guy, and he was old. My goal became not to quit Paxil before I ran out of it, but to quit Paxil while he was still around to help me.

He prescribed me more Paxil, but in the form of a liquid suspension, which meant that I would be able to measure smaller and smaller doses – down to the drop, and even smaller, because we could just keep increasing the dilution of the solution. It was brilliant.

It was a better idea than it tasted. I don't think I have ever had as much apple juice as I did in those three and a half months. It got the shit down.

Finally, nine months after I had taken it for the first time and eight months after I had decided to quit, I was free of Paxil.

I don't regret it. I learned to value incremental progress – something I probably would never have had the fortune to experience, had I not been forced into it. My usual M.O. is, "attack it obsessively until you either finish it or quit because it's taking too long" (and most things take too long).

You can't cure a drug dependency that way. You have to stay on schedule, and you can't jump ahead because chances are you'll be set back even further as a result. Patience and discipline will get you there, and that lesson is invaluable.

Still, I can't help but wonder if the entire situation could have been avoided.

Did I mention that this whole thing started because I thought there was something wrong with my heart?

AGE 22

I'm so afraid that
I'm going to lose myself
and find myself
at the same time.

July 4, 2004

Remember how I used to write about being afraid that I might be gay? Well, I'm NOT gay. I went through a time when I really wanted to be gay because I thought it would be easier than dealing with my intimacy issues and issues toward men. But I'm not gay, so I'm just going to have to deal with it. Just wanted to clear that up and put it in writing. You never know what might have happened if I died and the wrong people got their hands on this journal.

November 25, 2004

I won't lie - I have had crushes on girls - but I don't think they're crushes in the sense that I eventually want to sleep with them - it's more like I want a best friend. I also worry that all of this questioning automatically means that I'm gay, because don't straight people always know that they're straight?

Why is it so difficult? Sometimes they say that gay people always know that they're gay, but that doesn't fly for me, either. There are so many things about this that just confuse me. I do, however, know that I am scared shitless to find out that I'm gay. I don't know what I'd do with that. Run away and hide? I can't go to San Francisco; I have friends there. Ha.

I think there is a part of me that is curious to experiment. But I think that I'm first going to experiment on guys, because that's obviously easier and more convenient at this point.

November 27, 2004

I feel like I'm in this amazing, horrible, wonderful place of not knowing about anything right now. It's a feeling of powerlessness, and it's teaching me that what matters are not the things I view in the world, but how I view them. Really, that's the only thing we ever have control of. And it requires accepting that the answers don't come when we want them to. The answers come when the answers come.

December 8, 2004

How do you unlearn years of having to protect yourself from the people you were supposed to love, who were supposed to love you? How do you suddenly begin to live like the world is a safe place full of love? It's the hardest damn thing... ever.

December 14, 2004

I'm so tired again this morning, and I feel sort of icky. Icky like I'm lonely and I just want someone here with me - someone I can be physically close with and cuddle with. Or just sit really close to. I want someone to run their fingers through my hair and let me lie up against them. And the truth is, I don't care if it's a guy or a girl.

December 25, 2004

I realize now that if I want my life to change - if I want to welcome new things and people and experiences, I need to push past my fear. I need to do things even though I'm afraid of them. And the progress is in the action - in just doing it.

I love that I have the opportunity to do this right now. To let new things into my life - to try and to learn. And I have to remember that this is possibly so scary to me because it's so good - not because it's bad, and everything else I need to let fall into place.

December 29, 2004

The action is sometimes all it takes to turn something fake and awkward and scary into something that becomes second nature.

(In Hindsight)

IF YOU CAN'T SWIM, THE NILE IS NOT A RIVER.

There are things that I must eventually address. Like my seven-month relationship with a guy. A Man, you might say. And you would be correct.

His name was ●●●●, and we broke up three months before I came out. Neither of us was devastated. I guess I knew that was going to happen. He was part of my figurative dance between denial, self-discovery, regression, and more self-discovery.

Denial as a defense mechanism is underrated. It doesn't get as much publicity as arrogance or as much acceptance as humor. Maybe it's because arrogance and humor are defenses against others, while denial is a defense against yourself. I should know. Denial kept me safe from myself for quite a few years.

What you are about to witness is the breaking of that denial, which didn't come as much like a revelation or an epiphany as it did like a watched pot. You know – the kind that never boils, but eventually does? It was kind of like that, except... not as hot.

Anyway, I just thought I ought to warn you about the Man. Again, his name was ●●●●, although I haven't included much about him; partly because I didn't feel the need, and partly because I still respect him and value the time we spent together. We had each other for reasons, and I hope that I helped him to learn as much about himself as he helped me to learn about Me.

January 12, 2005

There's a small voice urging me to try kissing a girl. A weird thing, I feel, and for what purpose, I don't know, but the fact remains. There's not a girl in particular, just "a girl."

I don't know when or where I'd have the opportunity. I think if I ever found myself in an ideal situation, I'd have to go for it. I'd want to see what it's like, and to see if it would be mind-blowing. Anything mind-blowing I would be all for, because I ache to have my mind blown. It's probably what I want more than anything in the world.

I'm not quite sure why I'm writing about this in particular, except that I guess it's part of my creativity block, and if I want to unblock, I need to let myself unblock everywhere, and accept the thought that I might be interested in getting sexually satisfied by a girl. That could mean I'm gay, but it doesn't have to. It could simply mean that there's something emotionally that allows me to be that way with a woman and has me blocked for/from the same kind of pleasure with a man.

I need to keep an open mind. I won't paint myself into any kind of permanent picture or mold. That's not what life is about. Life is about exploration and change and taking risks and finding love. And sometimes love doesn't come without the other three. And the other three are kind of pointless without it. Isn't it funny how that stuff works? It's as if we try to keep ourselves from really living, and we have to be corrected every day.

January 20, 2005

I keep finding out that the things I thought would never happen to me are the very things that can and will. Sort of gives me a heads-up on what to watch for. Life is funny that way. Denial is funny that way.

I think that we don't fully realize the effects of denial - and when one is in it, there's really no easy way to get out. It's too bad that's how it works. Sometimes denial can be good. There are many things I'm sure would not have been accomplished if someone had not been in denial. In fact, most great things are accomplished by people whom others think are in denial - but the denial is actually of the possibilities.

February 1, 2005

To let others know me, and to trust that it will be okay, even if they decide that they no longer want to be my friend... That's what I worry about, about being gay - losing my friends. And I think that's what makes coming out so difficult - that to be yourself, you have to risk and know that not everyone will be there for you on the other side. At least, not in the way they were before.

There's a possibility that my relationship with ●●●● is something I need to do for myself in order to answer some questions about my sexuality.

I still feel the same way I did before. I have more desire to kiss a girl than a guy. I think I need to do some experimenting with girls in order to answer more questions and to satisfy this curiosity. This is the type of thing you want to be really sure about before you tell everyone.

February 19, 2005

I watched two more episodes of *The L Word*. It's a pretty good show. I like it. It's interesting because the main characters are lesbians living in Los Angeles, but I don't have any friends who would be interested in watching it or discussing it with me. At least I don't think so. Or maybe it's that I don't have any friends I'd be comfortable sharing my interest in it with. That's probably more like it.

●●●● watched a bit of it with me, but I think he feels threatened by my curiosity. He doesn't know it, but he should be. I don't want to hurt him, which is why I've held back certain things.

I don't know what I'd do if I all of a sudden found a girl I wanted to experiment with who also wanted to be with me that way. I think I'd have to go for it to find out for sure; to be able to live my life without any regrets. But isn't that true for anyone?

If you find someone who you think might fulfill you more, don't you owe it to yourself to pursue it in the name of happiness? Don't we each have that obligation to ourselves? I think we do, unless we're already invested in something through which the denial of this unexplored desire would in itself be fulfillment enough. That makes sense to me.

Choices are brutal because they become actions, and if you read actions, actions over words, the truth is always there.

February 23, 2005

Last night, I had a sexual dream about another female. I don't remember exactly what happened, but I remember that in the dream, I was absolutely certain of the fact that I was gay. Does that mean that I am gay, or was it just a crazy dream?

How do these things work? One thing I've become certain of is that I won't be able to rest on this issue until my curiosity has been satisfied. I know that someday I will kiss a woman. I don't know under what circumstances, but I know that it will happen. I've found those dreams arousing - and the thing that worries me is that I've never had them about men.

Part of my dream last night was about coming out, and it felt so good to be able to not care what everyone else thought. I wonder if my being gay would go against stereotype. Would I be one of those girls that no one would ever guess was gay? Or is everyone harboring a secret suspicion already that I am? I'll bet there were indications from as early as 12 years old, maybe earlier. Why am I pretending to be so confused?

February 28, 2005

The thing is, I want to be sexual with guys, but when it comes to sex with emotions, I think I'd be more comfortable with a girl. Does that mean I'm gay? What is sexual orientation, anyway? Does it define who you have sex with, or does it define who you love? I always thought it defined who you fall in love with - or that it was defined by that. In which case, maybe I'm a lesbian. How the fuck am I ever gonna find out? I don't know much except that for now, I just want to do what feels good.

March 5, 2005

I've come to the realization that I like dressing like a lesbian, which might lead people to think certain things about me, but isn't entirely bad. I think that I naturally have some good lesbian fashion sense, so the good news is, at least I have some kind of sense. I'd rather look like a fashionable lesbian than a straight girl who doesn't know what the hell she's doing.

March 13, 2005

I've been thinking about myself and my sexuality - how I'm now comfortable identifying myself as bisexual - at least to myself - and I wonder - how much of a difference is there between platonic love and romantic love - and what makes love romantic, since two people who love each other platonically can still have sex... and how does one tell? I don't know. I feel that I could fall in love with a woman.

March 18, 2005

My life seems right now to be devoid of any major difficulties...

We'd better knock on wood in case anyone or anything heard that utterly ridiculous statement. You know I didn't mean it.

AGE 23

I'm probably
a whole lot more powerful
than I think I am.

AGE 23

I'm probably
a whole lot more powerful
than I think I am.

May 31, 2005

There's something about the truth, and it's not only that it's liberating, although that's often the case. The truth is what brings about love. That's what I believe. If everyone lived true to themselves and to their relationships with others, we'd all be so much happier. Instead, the world isn't like that, and the most I can do is to show them myself and the way I want to experience and view the world, and hope that somewhere in there lies a connection.

Connection. Don't we spend most of our lives looking for just that? Whether it's physical or mental, we do - and most of the time, we don't even know what it is that we want to be connected to.

June 17, 2005

I'm still worried about being gay. Bisexual, I could handle. That's cool. But gay... that's a whole other thing.

I really am very happy with ●●●● - so why am I now wondering if there's something more passionate out there?

June 25, 2005

I find myself thinking more and more about experimenting sexually. With the same sex. What would it be like, and what would I find? If there is a part of me that belongs there, what will it take for me to be convinced? An actual physical experience, maybe. I think that if it's meant to happen, it'll happen.

I just wonder - would I be questioning it this much, at my age, if there wasn't anything there? Then again, I never went through a phase of experimentation, which is supposed to be perfectly healthy. Some people never need it, I know, but the way I was brought up, it's no wonder that I would be confused. Unfortunate, but no wonder.

One of the women I work with is a lesbian. I'd never actually known one who was out before, but ◊●◊●◊ is.

August 27, 2005

I'm seriously thinking about having sex with ●●●● this weekend. I just want to do it, find out what it's like, and then maybe every once in awhile we can get together and do it. I don't think it would be a bad idea. I guess what I do now is just call him and ask him to have sex with me. I hope he says yes. I'm going to be a little bit of devastated and angry if he says no. At this point, I'm not even so much worried about the pain. I just want to do it, already.

August 28, 2005

Last night, we tried to have sex, but it didn't quite work.

(In Hindsight)

I DIDN'T DO IT.

Before I came to my senses, I asked two guys to have sex with me. (Not at the same time.)

Neither of them worked out, which is fine, I guess. If there was a point where I should have been insulted, it was overridden by the fact that I didn't really want to have sex with either of them. I just wanted to get it over with. I wanted to be able to say that I had sex.

I have done other things. I know how powerful a blow-job can be. In a lot of ways, I think that blow-jobs are the universe's gift to people who sleep with men. Or maybe to people who are sleeping with men and don't really want to be. Or maybe just to men. Forget I said anything.

Let's back up a little.

I learned self-service when I was twelve or thirteen. It was completely intentional and not at all by chance. My seventh grade sex education class covered the topic of masturbation, and I thought, "How do you do that?" So I tried, wondering what the heck was supposed to happen, and I guess I caught on pretty quickly.

I did that for awhile with no outside help whatsoever, aside from a paragraph here and there in one of my teen romance novels.

Then, when I was fifteen, I discovered the online *X-Files* community. There is an incredible well of erotic fiction on the internet, the source of which is obsessed fans of mostly TV shows. I was a fan, and I liked to read. To be completely honest, that's where I learned most of what I know about sex.

For the first couple of years, I stuck to the Mulder/Scully pairing. Then I began to dabble in SlashFic, which is gay fiction in which Mulder is paired with another man, or Scully with another woman.

My self-service got a bit more interesting. And it was obviously satisfying enough.

The first time I kissed a boy, it was his birthday and the kiss was his present. We were 16, and we were standing on a lava rock cliff with the ocean crashing up against the rocks – if you can imagine. I remember thinking that any other girl would have been thrilled. I was simply uncomfortable.

At that point in my life, I had known for awhile that I liked girls. What I didn't quite grasp was what exactly it was that I was supposed to be feeling with guys.

When you've never been straight, you have no frame of reference for straightness. It took me awhile to figure out that what I felt for girls was what most girls felt for guys. (I would be in my early twenties before I made that connection.) And so I kissed him. Or I let him kiss me.

I went out with him for two months, and then didn't kiss anyone until I kissed him again, more than two years later, on the floor of my college dorm room.

(It was not for lack of opportunity that I remained a virgin. It was that I had no desire to *merge* with any of the boys I went on dates with.)

Four dry years after the floor kiss, curiosity got the better, and I would ask him to have sex with me. He would respectfully decline.

But within a few months after that, I had an actual boyfriend. He was basically my father, but I thought it was time to have sex.

Seven months later, we broke up. I had learned a lot of things. Sex was not one of them.

I did some re-evaluating. Where were my resources going? What was the critical path? How had I suddenly lost all interest in this venture?

Oh, yeah… I was gay. Always have been. Always will be.

September 25, 2005

So, have I really convinced myself that I'm gay? I have started to believe that I am. I'm actually more attracted to women than to men, but I don't know if I know how to deal with a woman's body below the shoulders.

I wonder if it would be a different story if I was actually with a girl and found her attractive and she wanted me to touch her. I wonder if that would make a difference. Maybe the fact that I want to kiss her hands and arms and shoulders and neck (and face) are just preliminaries - foreplay - and the rest will follow.

It's weird, dealing with this. I feel like I probably should have experimented in college. What did I do in college? I studied and I worked. I can't remember doing much else.

September 26, 2005

If you write gay fiction, does it mean that you're gay? Who would I be able to let read it? I think I need to write something like it - something that's not afraid to be honest. Maybe I'll find out what I like. Maybe I'll find that I have an easier time writing about this than I do about anything else. Maybe it doesn't even need to be that complicated. Maybe all it needs to be is "girl meets girl, and they fall in love."

October 4, 2005

If there's one person right now that I think I would benefit from spending more time with, it's ◊●◊●◊. She embodies for me the ideal that you can be who you are - not what everybody else is or thinks you should be - and still be largely powerful and successful in your life and in your career. The fact that she's gay only adds more experience to her credit, in my opinion. I could take a few lessons from observing.

October 6, 2005

What would I write if I wrote? I'm somewhat good at comedy, but I don't know. I had a crazy creative period about two years ago, and I've been dry ever since. Maybe there was freedom in that, and that scared me.

Maybe I need to admit to myself that I am probably gay and I need to live my life as such. I think the confusion is over how to handle the gay, not whether the gay is a fact. That's my experience, anyway.

It's definitely something that I want to explore. I can't be happy in the rest of my life until I experience for myself and stop wondering about what I might be missing. The fact that I wonder is enough. And someday, though it may never seem like the "right time" to come out, I will meet someone who makes it worth it.

I kept telling myself that I needed to have sex, just to do it once so I'd never have to do it again, and I still kind of feel that, but I know that I don't need to have sex with a man in order to know that I prefer women. Emotionally, that is. And physically, but I can't quite wrap my brain around what sex with a woman would actually be like. That's what's confusing to me. And if I'm not gay, where does all the other stuff come from? These are tough questions.

October 8, 2005

I want to make myself more conscious of the choices I make, of the paths that are in front of me. I can be happy with my life as long as I believe that everything is a choice - and even if it doesn't appear so, I still have a choice in how to react to things.

I can take it with grace. "Grace" is a great word, and it's something I'd like to achieve. Grace such that each action, each movement, seems conscious, even if it's not - well, not really that it seems conscious, but that it has a firm commitment behind it. I'm going to commit. Focus on the task at hand. Choose the moment.

If this doesn't make a difference in my life, I'll have to do some major, major searching. The kind of searching where you put all your stuff in storage and move out of your apartment and move to somewhere you don't know anyone.

How would I deal with being gay? It's weird because I know it; I do. I know that if I found the right woman, I'd be happier than if I was with a man. That is the truth as I know it right now. And yet... what am I waiting for? Waiting to establish myself, my success in other aspects of life, so at least I have some big things to my credit and feel financially secure? What if that day doesn't come, or what if I need to be open before those things happen?

Funny how I don't like to use the word "out." I like to use the word "open." What the difference is, I don't know. Ambiguity? Maybe.

On the other hand, though, I believe that things will happen when they're meant to happen, and so I don't need to worry about it. There's an element of free will involved, but most of it is the universe, I believe.

October 9, 2005

I've become obsessed with wondering how I should take action on the fact that I think I'm gay. Would it be so bad to tell people?

It's strange how, when I say that I'm attracted to a man, I feel like I'm lying. Most of the time. I mean, there are men that I like to look at, but it's just because I like to look at them; not because I find them sexy or have feelings for them.

It's different with women. I have feelings, and there are some occasions when I don't want to take my eyes off a particular person.

And we are so conditioned by society to think that heterosexuality is the biological way into which we all are born, that I continue to grasp at thin air, wondering whether something happened in my childhood to cause me to be this way. Was it my father? Was it some sequence of events that I don't remember? ...But then, I think, no... I was always attracted to women.

I've never been interested in girly things - I mean really girly things. Never liked wearing a dress; I've never owned or wore one that wasn't for a very special occasion - even skirts. Can't seem to wear make-up; can't seem to get away from my athletic shoes.

What if I was openly gay? What would happen? I'd have fewer straight female friends to hang out with. What I'm hoping is that everyone already sort of knows. That it's not a complete surprise.

How do I fit in as a lesbian, I wonder? I think I'm somewhere in the middle. Most people are somewhere in the middle. Luckily, I'm in Los Angeles, where every other person is gay, it seems. Just all of my friends aren't.

So I like girls. So I'm going to have to change my life. So I'm going to be happy. So I'm already pretty happy.

October 11, 2005

I want to feel the excitement of liking someone who likes me. I want to smile at a glance - to feel my insides dance in a way that makes me want to grin from ear to ear. A feeling you can't talk about but to say, "Wow."

I wonder if I'll ever have that kind of a relationship with a girl. I don't think I ever have or ever will with a guy. A guy has never made me want to - or be willing to - try things I've never done before. The leaps I take are for girls. That's probably an indication.

October 12, 2005

I look at peoples' hands, and I rarely like peoples' hands. But occasionally, there's someone whose hands I do like, and when that happens, I start to think about physical intimacy and how that might be nice. I guess hands are important because I want someone whose hands I can play with - whose hands I'm excited to have touch me.

I wonder if gay women have sort of a vibe about me, like – "She might be." I have so many characteristics and things about my life that would point to my being gay - it would make more sense than my being straight.

How would I come out? Who would I tell? I wonder if any of my friends are also gay. I have so many friends who are girls, none of whom are gay, and I wonder sometimes how I ended up so out of my demographic. Statistically, though, I must know other lesbians. They just might not be out, yet. A lot more people are gay than I thought.

October 19, 2005

I have no desire to suck ●●●●'s dick, anymore. But how do I tell him something like that? How do I tell him that I'm most likely gay? That would suck - to be on the receiving end of that news. Geez.

October 19, 2005

I feel alone. Sometimes the choice is preferable to the choice to not be alone.

If I could have anything in the world, what would I want?

October 28, 2005

I'm watching *The L Word* right now. It's a good show. It's smart, funny, and fucking sexy. It's a show about friendship. Well-written, well-acted, well-executed in general. It's a show I'd love to work on. It's ground-breaking, really.

I guess I'm finally coming to terms with the fact that I'm not straight. I was about to say "entirely straight," but that simply means that I'm not straight. I don't know exactly how to define what I am, and I don't think that I have to. I think deep down, where there is no fear, I know that I'm gay. I am gay. I am so gay. I have been forever.

I'm interested in and attracted to other lesbians - the energy and chemistry there - something that's not present with any of the guys I've come across. With guys, it's been circumstantial, but the way I've felt about girls, even if there was no reciprocation…

There were feelings that I had to hide, for fear of being rejected. I don't like that fear. I want to show how I feel for someone without having to hide it - without being afraid. I want to experience the physicality - the wonder of touching and being touched by someone who excites me - who I physically desire. Someone I just really, really want. Who I feel like would blow my mind if I got to be with. Someone who felt the same about me.

I have a sort of masculinity that I feel strongest when I'm around very girly girls - I feel somehow that I'm lacking in femininity. And I look at them, and I think, I don't want to *be* that; I want to *have* that.

Weird. But look at me being honest with myself.

October 29, 2005

All right. So. Do I have a responsibility to live my life any differently because I believe I'm gay? It still feels like a lie to go on letting myself be known as straight. I mean, it's not something you can really hide when people know you, so I'm sure that everyone probably already has their suspicions - which almost makes it worse.

You know what? I'm not going to worry about it because the time will come when it does. Something that interests me is how much it makes a difference that there are more gay characters and people in the media. It really helps society accept the difference as "okay."

I believe it's essential for us to study and understand human nature - because then we understand ourselves and we realize that the next guy's no different, and we have more tolerance because wouldn't we want someone else to have tolerance for us, too?

October 30, 2005

I'm getting closer and closer. Don't know how it's going to happen or when, but I'm getting there. At least I'm thinking about it - I have these moments when I think that it would be totally simple and just okay for me to tell everyone, and then I have moments when I'm completely terrified - not of telling them, but of what their reactions will be. And I realize that I'm trying to set my life up so that I can be self-sufficient, should my friends and family choose to abandon me. I'm fine with it - if they don't like it, I'd prefer that they stay away. But it's still sad.

November 7, 2005

Yesterday, one of my neighbors asked me out. He's a guy that I see on the elevator, every once in awhile. I've had maybe three conversations with him. Well, he knocked on my door and gave me some cookies and asked me out to dinner. I panicked, told a lie - that I was kind of seeing someone - and felt like a total asshole because I don't even remember this guy's name.

It's very weird to me - this is the first time I've been asked out by someone who doesn't know me. And that shocks me because I'm not a girly-girl; I don't put a lot of time and effort into my physical appearance. I don't try to look good in the context of attracting guys or competing with other women. I just wear what I want to and am as low-maintenance as I want to be. So it really surprises me when something like that happens because it's not even something that I ever think about.

And after he left, I sat at my desk, holding the cookies - which were still warm from baking - and I thought, "This has got to stop." This has got to stop, if only so these guys don't keep thinking that they have a chance. I sat there with the cookies and felt so guilty. And now I'm going to have to return the container that he brought the cookies in.

Why do I feel so awkward in these situations? And he seems like a very nice guy - that's what makes it worse. But I'm not attracted to him, and I don't think I ever will be, so there's no possibility, in my mind, for a date or anything that might typically come out of a date.

This thing about my sexuality has become sort of an obsession. It's always in my mind, and I know that I'm going to have to start telling people. Who do I tell? Everyone, I guess. But in what order?

November 8, 2005

I'm so close, and yet now I'm backpedaling because of ●●●●. It's like my brain is saying, "You're not totally gay. What about ●●●●?"

Then again, we were together for seven months, and I had no problem holding off on the sex part of the relationship - I mean, there was making out, but I really had no actual desire for sex, other than curiosity. And it was like I always let him take the lead because I wasn't really into initiative, which I think would be different if I was with a girl. I think my sense of initiative would be much stronger with a girl.

What the fuck does it all mean? Especially when I don't want guys' attention

- I just want them to keep the fuck out of my personal space - but then I try to get closer to girls.

I'm so gay. I'm so gay and I'm trying to find a way out of it. I've had crushes on girls forever. Have I just been so conditioned by society to think that I should be looking for a guy? I think so. And my brain still tries to find ways to keep me in there.

But even when I was with ●●●●, I knew it was to find out what sex was like and probably never date another guy in my life - so what can I say? Not much except that I think I'm gay.

Once I come out and say it, I don't think there will be a question. In other words, the only thing keeping me from feeling the truth is denial of that truth. I need to have the guts to go with my gut. Think about what I could do - where I could go. Can't worry about what everyone else will think. That will only lead to driving myself crazy.

November 10, 2005

Do I have a responsibility to all of mankind to be who I am? Here's the better question – Do I have a responsibility to all of mankind to let it be known who I am? Everything I am?

I believe that I have a responsibility not to lie. I'm not going to tell a lie about who I am. But withholding information, isn't that an entirely different thing? Don't we each also have a right to privacy, to protect things inside until we are ready for the world to see them? I think we do. And I'm not ready.

Well, maybe I am; I mean I know I'm ready to take little steps. I'm just not ready to announce it to everyone I know, just yet. I think that's fair, and I don't think that anyone will judge me for having kept that private while I did. I have finally accepted the fact that I will probably never have sex with a man. I'm just not emotionally invested enough.

"The key is accepting yourself."

*(Valuable advice from the first person
I ever came out to.)*

ZOE
Hey. Hey - it's okay.

HALEY
I know you think so. But what if it's not?

ZOE
What if it's not okay? Listen, Haley, there will always be people who rag on everything they don't understand or can't relate to - and it's because they don't _want_ to understand. Which is their loss. Don't let it be yours. Just... Whatever makes you happy, okay? It's all right. And fuck everyone who thinks it's not.

COMING OUT

I thought that everybody already knew and was waiting for me to come out of the closet. I guess it's like how you could feel really nervous but then people are like, "You were? I couldn't tell."

I believe my exact words were, "Scared shitless."

November 11, 2005

I did it. Wow. I came out to ◊●◊●◊. One person, and already I feel different.

There's really no going back on it. The great thing is that I don't think I'd ever want to – go back on it, I mean.

The challenge is finding the guts to let everyone else know. But I took the first step, which feels good. Really good.

It's funny how people put so much on the sexual aspect – the physicality – when really, the thing that tells me I'm gay is that I become emotionally invested in females.

So there's initial attraction, a crush, a hope, and the intense desire to learn all you can about the person. That's who we end up loving and what determines a life partner – not the sex. The sex is secondary.

Sex and romantic love are two entirely different things. Ideally, they're inseparable and don't contradict each other. But you can definitely have one without the other. That's what makes it difficult for people who aren't straight – and why, to those who don't get it, it seems like people have a "choice."

To be happy in this case…in this case, you don't get to choose who or what makes you happy. It just is.

I believe that everything happens when it's going to happen. You can't make things happen; you can only recognize an opportunity when it comes along.

I'm okay; I'm doing just fine. The reality is that I'm probably going to lose a few friends. And maybe my family will never acknowledge me. But I'll be true to myself.

November 12, 2005

I just want to fall in love – that's all. To fall madly, hopelessly in love. I want to create a home with that person; to be cozy. Really, that's all I want in this life – to be cozy with someone. I'll find it. Have to be patient – with myself and with others.

I often wonder what it would be like to be completely free, emotionally. To feel while taking part in sex. To truly make love. I'll find out.

I'm learning to have faith in the universe, in circumstance. Things happen when they're going to happen. And what's funny is that you never know what's about to change, or why.

November 13, 2005

Yesterday, I got my first "real" haircut. It cost $50 and I walked out with $50 of product on top of that, but I felt good about the whole experience. I'm waking up to myself. I feel like I want to be attractive.

I'm glad that I've gotten a lot more comfortable with the word "lesbian." I used to not really be able to say the word, and it's still a little difficult saying it in reference to myself, but it's not quite as big of a deal anymore.

I'm still having problems with the phrase "coming out," I don't know why; maybe because it sounds so gay?

The next person to figure out who to tell is my mom. She'll probably tell the whole rest of the family. Will it be my "best friend" that I bring home for a visit, or will they acknowledge her as the person I love and want to share my life with?

I just don't want all the questions that I know people are going to ask. I just want them to take it in and say, "Okay." Or if they would just say, "Oh, okay. Yeah, we kind of figured." That would be the best response I could get. The worst would be a complete dismissal of the subject never to be brought up again.

There are so many people that I need to talk to about it that it seems an impossible task. I have a feeling that I'm going to tell some people over e-mail. With my friends from high school and college, there's not a better way to do it. I think they would probably prefer if I did it over e-mail.

November 14, 2005

I'm eager to tell everyone, and at the same time I dread it. I'm guessing that when I start telling people, I'm going to feel horribly exposed and maybe even a little violated. It's necessary, though, to get through to the other side.

There are probably many implications that I haven't even thought of, yet. I know I'll be fine, though.

But now I'm also afraid of dating, you know? Of getting emotionally invested in someone who doesn't want what I want. It was never a really big risk with guys, because I wasn't invested and always enjoyed my time away without another thought to them.

November 15, 1005

I feel like I need to touch base with someone to whom I can talk with no fear – I need to feel like I have some support. And I can't beat myself up about it. I need to accept the care of the people around me, for once. Let them help me. Let myself want that help. I don't need to do everything by myself. I don't mean in the literal sense; I mean in the figurative, emotional sense. I can let people be there for me. Admit that I'm afraid.

November 16, 2005

Have you ever been so hurt by someone that even though they're still a big part of your life, there are things that you no longer want them to see? And the things don't even have to be bad; they can be good things, too. But you just don't want to share, anymore.

That's how I feel about telling my parents that I'm gay. I feel like they must already know – how could anyone who really knows me – not know? Then again, who really knows me?

I can't care about the fact that people will be talking about me. I haven't cared about what people have thought of my decisions up to this point. I've always found a way to do what I want to do, and this isn't going to be any different.

November 18, 1005

I still don't understand why I need to say out loud something that everyone should already know. It seems cruel. Actually, I do understand why – it's because people generally don't want it to be true.

It feels so good to be able to admit to myself what this is, and to be able to articulate what it is that makes my feelings toward girls different than my feelings toward guys.

About other people, though – maybe I'm looking at it backwards – like, what if people never wanted to say anything because they thought that I would take offense? That's entirely possible, and when I do come out, those same people may feel as if they've been lied to. I need to be sensitive to that, as well.

November 19, 2005

◊●◊●◊ and I went to lunch and talked. Talking was surprisingly easy. And it was amazing to share thoughts and experiences with someone who has had them too. About this. And she made me feel okay about not broadcasting to the world, but not hiding, either. Just being. And I think that's what I'm going to do. I'm just going to be.

November 20, 2005

You know what's awesome? The fact that since I've begun to accept myself as gay, my ability to fantasize has come back. It's like I'm now allowing myself to have all these thoughts and feelings that I had been afraid to confront – and I can imagine again. I can imagine things in the context of my own life and in make-believe.

How wonderful is it that I can let myself fantasize about a girl and get turned on? It's amazing. I can't even explain the freedom I feel inside.

And I suddenly have more confidence about myself and my place in the world, and me as a unique person, an artist, and a catalyst for change – with the power to affect the lives of others. And yet I know that I don't want to make any grand gestures, as of yet. All I want to do is to work on my life and do what I want to do, and make myself happy. That's all.

November 21, 2005

I'm a little obsessed with the gay thing, but I guess that's to be expected. Knowing that I am is one thing, but the fact remains that I still haven't spoken about it with my family or friends, and I don't have any gay friends (there's ◊●◊●◊, but I don't want to become a parasite), which I'm finding is a major deal to me.

I just have a lot of work to do on my life. I consider it work because it will involve meeting new people and trying to become their friend. Want to hurl just thinking about it.

November 22, 2005

I think I'm having a tough time with the fact that I don't have any gay friends. Outside of work, that is. It's really, really tough, especially now that I've talked about it out loud – with just one person, but all of a sudden it became real, and I don't want to keep my life on hold like it's been.

I just realized, you know – I'm not going to find what I'm looking for in the friends I have now, no matter how great they are. They're never going to really understand or be able to relate to me in that sense, and why should they – look how difficult it's been, so far. *I* can't relate to *them*.

Talking about it with ◊●◊●◊ was like the most natural thing in the world to me. Felt great to be able to use the word "she" or "her" in a sentence without feeling like people would pick up on something.

November 23, 2005

I can't wait to fall in love. I've not felt this way before; maybe because I always truly wanted something different than what everyone else was telling me that I should want. Becoming conscious of that was like, "Duh." Of course. I want to be with a girl. I want to fall in love with a girl who wants to fall in love with me. I have no idea where I'm going to find her or who she's going to be. But I all of a sudden feel like the chances of finding her are infinitely greater than those of finding the guy I thought I was supposed to find. Isn't that funny? It's hysterical – but I guess that's what the difference is.

This is bittersweet because all of a sudden, I feel like I'm living a life I've created, but not for myself - it was for this other person who doesn't exist anymore. And I need to start listening to me.

November 24, 2005

I've decided that I'm not lying anymore. I'm not going to lie. I'd rather stay silent than lie. That, to me, is an important step. Because I believe that if you stop lying, it isn't long before the truth just naturally appears. It doesn't even need to be prompted – it just appears. I need to trust that it will, in this case.

"The truth will out," as they say. I wonder if the people who made that saying popular were gay. Nah, it's probably another one of those things that comes from the Bible. I'm still reading it – only to de-mystify it. I've even stuck a post-it note that says this on the cover, in case anyone finds it.

November 26, 2005

I spent today at Disneyland. It was fun. I usually get this deep sense of dread at being out of control and helpless on a ride. It's fear of what could happen, and I hadn't yet figured out a way to beat it. Until today.

I asked myself, what's scarier – going on this ride, or having to deal with everyone I know when I finally come out? So, I went on all the rides. That really helped, because I can think of few things that are more terrifying than having to face everyone in my life with the fact that I am gay.

I've decided to take more risks and let more of who I truly am shine through, and there has been a difference in the way I face the world. Right now, though, it's kind of like I'm plowing on through because I don't want to lose my nerve for anything.

November 27, 2005

Life's weird. I still am who I am to my friends, but I guess I'm not who I am to myself, anymore. That makes sense, I suppose. It's like I finally stop trying to kid myself, and all of a sudden, I have the responsibility to myself to be who I am. I feel like I've been selling myself out for my whole life, and now I'm waking up to realize that following my truth is a much better way to go.

It's tough to suddenly not care what people think of me. I'm trying to create a disconnect there, because in the past I've judged myself on how I lived up to others' expectations – or I created my own expectations around those of others, and got frustrated when they didn't match up to who I really am.

All this sounds crazy, but to me, nothing has made more sense. And it's all about action and the moment and what happens now.

I can't stop thinking about what it would be like to have gay friends – I mean girls, not guys. I feel like I would just be so much more comfortable. Maybe that's just wishful thinking. I just know that knowing that I share this with them would make me feel safer – and not just inside. It's like I'd feel a kind of underlying connection – a bond or something like that. Something that allows us to communicate with silence and mere presences – the act of companionship which I've never really felt before. I mean, not in this context.

It is so weird and frightening to me, this fact that I don't have any lesbian friends. I keep wondering how and why the fuck it happened like this. I mean, usually when you're 23 and ready to come out, it's because you already have gay friends, if only through circumstance, right? Well, all of my circumstantial friends are straight. And I don't know where to go to find lesbians who would want to be my friends.

November 28, 2005

It just turned cold the day before last, and it finally feels like wintertime. I like it, and I don't. I like it because it makes me feel like being cozy. I don't like it because I don't yet have anyone to be cozy with. I get why so many babies are conceived in the winter. Wow.

I truly feel like I'm living a life I created for someone else. I'm not what my life is. I never was, but I'm only now realizing who I actually am. It's empowering, and I no longer feel like I need to justify myself to anyone. That's a very good thing. A step forward in itself. I know what I want, at least. And I know that my feeling of not belonging isn't something that's wrong inside of me. It has nothing to do with my being introverted or "anti-social." I feel different because I am, and it's simply what is. Nobody can change it. Nobody can change it, so the way to be happy is to approach it from a different angle. Be brave.

I already am brave; I think the rest of my life has been a precursor to all of this. I can't help but feel that way. At least I feel somewhat prepared.

I wonder how I fooled myself for so long. I didn't even realize what I was doing. I guess that's how susceptible I was to outside influences, in that respect. I just sort of acted how people expected or how I thought that people expected me to act. But I didn't want to date boys. I couldn't see any happiness there for me, even though I've been asked out by plenty of guys.

Now that I've begun to come out, I can see happiness – the potential for it – even though I don't know anyone and I'm pretty far, it seems, from my first date with a woman. It's something I want to do, and that's an entirely new feeling for me in this context. It's wonderful, and it just makes me want to be quiet and imagine and smile – daydream.

November 29, 2005

Of course I would have to be gay, right? Of all of life's challenges, why should I be spared that one? It's totally funny and cosmic and just completely me. That would be me. Things work out, I guess. Eventually.

November 30, 2005

I had a moment last night that was reminiscent of the moment I had when my neighbor showed up at my door with cookies – the moment in which I realized the guy never had a chance, and no guy, really, ever had a chance, and I knew why they never had a chance.

My moment last night was when I realized that people were probably going to keep acting like I thought I was straight until I let them know that I know that I'm gay. The moment in which I mentally threw my hands up and said, "This has got to stop." I have a feeling that a lot of things are going to be like that.

December 1, 2005

Things are simple, yet complicated. Isn't that how it always is? I didn't tell ◊●+●◊ yesterday, like I was going to. Guess I will today, because my "girliness" came into question again yesterday. It was actually the perfect opening.

I think the problem is that I have no idea how they're going to react. I don't know how to brace myself for what's coming. That may be good, because then I'm more likely to be honest, whatever follows. They won't be shocked that I'm gay; they might be shocked that I've said it. Two entirely different things.

I'm actually not doing too badly, considering I'm 23, and I wasn't even ready to be sure I was gay until I broke up with ●●●●. Isn't that funny? I dated him because I wanted to see what sex was like, but we broke up before it happened.

And then I realized that the thought of finding another guy that I could stand to have sex with was something I just wasn't interested in putting any time and effort into. That was probably my strongest indication. I didn't feel any kind of excitement inside when I thought about dating more guys.

Even though I had fun fooling around with ●●●●, I just didn't have the kind of emotional connection with him that I feel when I have a crush on a girl. It's completely different. It feels like there's nothing I want more than just to be with this person.

I've only felt that feeling when it wasn't reciprocated. I don't know what it's like to be in love with someone who's in love with me. I know what it's like to NOT be in love with someone who's in love with me. That's not too fun. I have a feeling there will be more of the former and less of the latter, going forward.

Now I know what I want. And I think I had it backward. It might be more logical for me to come out at work, then my friends, then my family. That would be easier for me, probably, and who says I shouldn't make it as easy as I can?

I feel like what I have inside isn't as much a fire as it is a glowing piece of charcoal. A fire would be too obvious.

IN)SANITY LETTERS: PART I

PERFECTION

I turn myself into a character and I write a story and that's how I tell the truth because the truth needs less courage that way and I can claim that it's part of the character and the story is fiction but some truths don't lose my voice. Some truths are too real and one feels that the difference is obvious between what is imagined and what is reality, unless one is writing of something that was imagined in reality; a fantasy or a daydream based on the truth of real life, and where does imagination become a different thing than fantasy? When is each? I imagine things, and when I wish them to happen, we call it fantasy – and when I don't wish them to happen, we call it worry; anticipation.

There are both, when I think of you. I think of you, and the moment expands. I have a sphere which I don't otherwise notice, invisible to others but appears to me with a thought of you, and the thought becomes the center of the universe, but inside my head, so I turn inward and become blind and deaf so I am not conscious of seeing or hearing what, seconds ago, was the world. Now it's my world and the obsessiveness of thought is enough to exhaust me and I wonder why it is that I shut down and feel I must be alone.

I don't think you know what it would be like to have me love you. Neither do I. I imagine sometimes that you'd invite me to your place, and you move over so that I am within reach and find an excuse to make me close the gap – and all of a sudden I find that you are closer even than my fantasies, and all I need is the courage to act because maybe it's you who is waiting for me, and not the other way around as I would have myself believe. Although, in the end, I have a notion that it is most perfect when two people have been waiting for each other.

I've never known perfection. What I've known are the motions – the physical act of relationship, whereby one does all the things that one believes such a relationship would entail, knowing all the while that there must be something more. That there must be a point – and the irony is to realize that perfection is letting go of the point. Perfection in love, that is, not in the mathematical sense. Perfection is the means as an end.

December 2, 2005

I came out to ◊●+●◊ and ◊+◊+◊, yesterday. It was tough – it had taken me a couple of days to find the "perfect moment," and even then, it took me what felt like forever to actually get it out.

It was kind of fun and very nerve-wracking, but not as scary as I thought it was going to be. There was a moment of nakedness that I felt as I was telling them, but talking about it was pretty easy. So it's just getting past that moment of nakedness that I need to bear. Because once that's over, it's been done and there's no taking it back. NO taking it back.

It's like ripping off a Band-Aid, except that you can't put it back on if you decide you made a mistake. Well, I guess you can't put a Band-Aid back on, either. They don't stick as well. So, yes – it's just like ripping off a Band-Aid.

Exposing myself. I have a feeling that this will make a difference in my life. I hope it will make it easier for me to tell my friends and family. That's the bitch – once you've been honest with yourself, you want to keep being honest, and that means letting certain people know certain things.

I guess I'm really good at keeping private. I didn't realize I hide so much. I'm just a hider – it's become my nature because of the way I grew up, I guess. Maybe now that will change – or maybe everyone will find out that I haven't been hiding anything – my life is just fairly simple and boring. Actually, I don't think it's boring, but others might. I like my life. I have a feeling that I'm about to like it even more.

I can't believe I'm doing this – I'm so proud of myself. The thing is, I can't stand the thought of NOT doing this.

December 3, 2005

Came out to •+•+•, yesterday. He didn't believe me, at first. I knew that I was going to have to explain how I knew, and I'm finding that I really don't have a problem with that, as long as people accept what I tell them.

I wonder when I actually knew that I was probably gay. I think I started considering that I might be in the eighth grade. I had a few crushes on girls, that year. It's tragic how tough it is for many people to figure this thing out about themselves, because accepting it is even tougher, and coming out is probably one of the hardest things we've ever had to do. I'm okay, though. I'm doing okay.

December 4, 2005

Last night, I found that I wasn't yet ready to tell =◊=. And I didn't feel like I had failed in any way. It was okay. I may need to write a letter or an e-mail. And that would be okay.

I'm coming to terms with a lot of things, including the fact that there will be some people that I just won't tell. Not directly, anyway. And it's not a bad thing. It's protecting myself, which is okay. It's okay.

All I need to do is to be happy. I'm beginning to understand that, now. There are people who I want to tell, and will. All I need to do is to make tiny changes in the direction of my happiness. Everything else will work itself out.

December 5, 2005

My life is so new to me. It's like I'm experiencing so many things for the first time. I sound dramatic, but it's really true. There's something truly amazing about suddenly having knowledge about yourself that makes you look at everything in a whole different way. Maybe not different, but with a new understanding.

I used to be so bitter and angry as a result of feeling different. Now I know why. I know why. And even though I'm not nearly where I want to be, at least I know what I want. Not getting frustrated with getting there is the challenging part. But now that I know what was causing my frustrations, I don't really have an excuse. I just need to suck it up. And I'm going to be so proud of myself.

And so happy. I already am. I am probably twice as happy now that I've admitted to myself and a few other people that I'm gay. It's tougher for others to upset me.

When I think about the fact that I've told people, I still feel utterly exposed and vulnerable, but I can't waste time thinking that way. I can't undo it. I can't take it back, and why should I want to? So I'd have to do it all over again? Every time I get scared about coming out, I think about how my life has been, versus how it could be, and there's really no question. If I want to be happy, there is no choice.

December 6, 2005

Sometimes, it's tough to see the light at the end of the tunnel. I feel like there are skylights along the way, but still. I'm so far from where I want to be. Good to have challenges, I guess. People look at me and what I allow them to see, and it must appear as though I have a boring life. I'm never bored, though. I keep things interesting for myself. I'm always working on myself; how can that be boring? I guess for those who are well-adjusted, there's not much to work on. I'm always striving, though. I've got time to do things, provided that I don't die a tragically early death. That would suck.

December 9, 2005

Knowing who you are is a blessing and a curse. On the one hand, you know who you are. A good thing. On the other hand, it saddles you with this obligation to live your life true to yourself, just because you're conscious of what is true to yourself.

Ugh, I'm such a social failure.

December 10, 2005

Anxiety, fear, confusion, anger, resentment, frustration, a wall between me and happiness – a place I want to be, so far, at the end of a long journey. Courage. Truth.

Living the truth is difficult, a challenge. Living the truth is infinitely more difficult than living what others want from you; giving in to their perceptions and letting them mold who you are. I don't want that.

I want what I want, and I want to be like those successful people around me.

"Successful" might be the wrong word, though. I just mean that I'm grateful for the good fortune or privilege or blessing to be able to observe and be around people who I can use as an example – role models. Someone that you relate to enough and with whom you have enough things in common that it's reassuring to you to see that they're already a step or two steps or three in the direction that you want to go. Because then, really all you have to do is to follow. And if you have the intelligence to choose the right people, the following is not an act of conformity but a necessary exploration of the truths within yourself.

I have the privilege to have such people in my life, and if not for them, I would have found myself on an entirely different path. There is always that other path, but the key is finding one on which you are so happy that you don't care to think about the others. That's living your truth.

Living the truth. Being honest about yourself and what's inside of you. Not stopping when fear hits. Being willing to go there. My problem is that I'm not sure exactly where "there" is. I don't know what all of these negative feelings are shielding. Maybe it's just me. And maybe I really am no different than everyone else.

Everything is a choice, and all I have to do is to choose to look at things in a certain light – that scary things are more like challenges that I'll be proud of myself for overcoming. That there are many worse things in the world, and I can create obstacles for myself, or I can find solutions to overcome the obstacles that are not in my control. Action. Still have work to do there, but I've been doing a good job, so far.

December 11, 2005

You know, I just want to experience flirting with someone that I want to flirt with, who might actually want to flirt with me. I don't think I've had that experience before. I'm 23, and I've never had that experience before.

December 12, 2005

This is really a little nerve-wracking – trying to date and find new friends. At least I'm not that insecure about myself. I have a much better self-image regarding being a lesbian than I do about being a straight girl. That, to me, is a relief.

December 16, 2005

You know what's funny – that lesbians have this reputation of being rough and not being afraid to be bitchy – and I mean, maybe to some extent, it's true. But really, there's a softness and a vulnerability under all that, that is beautiful, and in my mind, unequaled by any other gender personality.

I guess I just want someone to be that way with me, and me with them. Someone I can talk softly to on the phone – who, when people hear, they know who it is because my voice changes and I go all soft. Wouldn't that be wonderful?

IN)SANITY LETTERS: PART II

IMAGINARY

You go to work, home, and sleep. Did you know that there are two of you? The other lives in my head. It seems I made her, but I don't own her; don't control her – because I like it when she surprises me. She is quiet for a time and then reminds me that to everything there is another layer, an element, and like looking through a filter, I see things in terms of you.

For some I have no frame of reference; no established knowledge of the way you would react, but she takes a guess and I remind myself to check with you to find out if she is right. She gets better the more I know you. But still, I'm not sure and I don't trust her responses to things I want to tell you but never have. I won't consult you on these, and I fear that she is wrong, and I notice a trend – sometimes, all things being equal, she tells me what I want to hear.

I am suspicious, because as a tenant of my mind, she has reason to lie. And because I want you near, I have reason to believe. But I remember that it's not you who is answering, though she looks like you, sounds like you, smiles like you, and I can't touch her, either. Both of you – mysteries to me. With her, I fill in the blanks.

If you were here, she'd leave and I'll know less than I thought I did and I don't care. I will relearn; I will overwrite. I will accept truth.

December 17, 2005

There are some people who seem to get hit on everywhere they go – I'm not one of them, or I haven't been. I hope I look like a lesbian. How am I supposed to get other girls to ask me out, otherwise?

December 18, 2005

I have a feeling that when I tell my family and friends from high school, it'll be like breaking through some kind of a sound barrier.

I'm really grateful for this, actually. I'm grateful because in being forced to confront such a thing, the courage it'll take for me to face other things pales in comparison. My frame of reference has been blasted wide open, and I'm not as afraid of the stupid things that I always was afraid of – like speaking up. Because what is there to say that is more nerve-wracking and requires more courage than, "I'm gay"? There are not many things, let me tell you.

…Oh, god…I'm really gay.

December 20, 2005

Came out to ●◊+◊● last night, over the phone. It took me so much guts to actually say it; to start off the "gay" conversation. That's always the hardest part, and then the actual talking about the gaiety is fairly easy for me. Except that I'm still a bit uncomfortable about certain words. I think that a lot of people are, though.

I'm just happy about making progress. Not that I need to keep telling more people in order for it to qualify as progress, but I'm going to have to do it eventually, so why not push forward? We brought up an interesting point, last night – I'm not so afraid of telling my friends from high school, but I'm sort of worried about how their parents will react. Stuff could get really weird. I don't want stuff to be weird for my parents, but in some ways I don't see that there's really any way around it. I have to do what I have to do – what makes me happy.

I know there will be consequences for my family and friends, but they can choose how they want to think and what they want to do with it. And I will also need to respect that, too. I have to be prepared to be sensitive to the feelings of others – they are likely to be way more unprepared for this than I am, because I'm the one who has been thinking about it for so long. The first they're hearing about it might be when I tell them, and that can sort of be a shock to a person. Especially if they never even entertained the possibility before.

I'm finding, though, that maybe I'm not as obvious as I thought I was – but it's also this extreme bias that society has against homosexuality – "straight until proven gay" is the way that most people look at it. All you have to do, most of the time, is to act like you believe that you're straight, and most of the time people will accept you as such. I sorta wish that everyone already knew, because then I wouldn't feel like they had to get used to the idea.

December 21, 2005

I need to have some courage. Grow some balls. Stand up and claim my happiness. Sometimes, I feel lost and so… just lost and lonely. And I wonder – how is it ever going to change? How is it ever going to be different? And the answer, duh, is – I'll make it different.

December 22, 2005

I'm almost halfway out, by now. A few more people, and I will be halfway out. Actually, the full way out.

My goal is to be out to pretty much everyone by the new year. I'm so looking forward to being totally out. I sort of want the whole world to know. I sort of want the whole world to know *me*. Wouldn't that be amazing?

Looking back on things, I see now where I could have seen so clearly. You know? Like the questions to ask myself to determine whether I was gay – but the truth is, I knew for a long time. It was just a matter of admitting to myself that I knew.

It was always easy if I chose for it to be easy. It's like that with a lot of things – with most things, actually. I'm scared of a lot of things. I'm losing perspective – or I do lose perspective, often. I need to take my own advice and grow some balls. Have some courage, and some faith.

December 26, 2005

I know with certainty that someday, I will be out to everyone in my life. Especially if I have someone special in my life – a girlfriend. I'll be so happy; so proud – how can I even think of keeping that all in? There's no way. And I can't wait for it to happen.

December 29, 2005

I'm becoming conscious of things that have so far kept me from doing the things I want to do – from being the person I am.

Who am I? Who the fuck am I? I always, always, maintained that if there was one thing I knew, it's who I am. I thought I knew. I swore I wasn't one of those teenagers who rebels under the guise of trying to figure out who I am. "Stupid," I thought. "That's for lost kids who just want attention."

Well, I'm 23 and almost 24, and I'm going to be right in the middle of figuring it out. It's not a joke or a cry for attention. It just feels damn good. It feels good to find truth – to find a piece of something that you know is you.

I am excited, because it's just as much creating who I am as finding out who I already am. How do you figure it out? Who knows? Take nothing for granted. I'm ready to admit that I have no idea who I am.

I think it takes a bit of courage and a lot of determination to uncover truth. The great thing is that some truths are simple and are just a matter of me standing up for rights that I've always known that I should have. Simple as that. Simpler said than done, though.

January 3, 2006

I've talked about being gay; now what I want to talk about is my attraction to girls – the crushes I've had and the crushes I have, and who and what I'm generally attracted to. Something that straight people get to talk about all the time, right?

Why is it so tough? Why must we make the choice, every day, between what we reveal and what we keep secret? I mean, everybody has to do that, to some extent, but gay people have to do it more often. In everyday conversation.

Coming out is going to be a life-long process, it appears. I had hoped that people already knew, but that's not the case.

I take comfort in reading books on this, though, because it shows me that the ways I think and feel are shared by an entire community of people, albeit a scattered community. The ways I think – the logic – are not mine, alone. My arguments for issues – I'm not alone in my beliefs. And at the same time, I realize even more that there is a fundamental difference between gay people and straight people. We're just not going to think the same. And the views of gay people have not yet been accepted by American society. Or by any society.

January 3, 2006

I can't wait to have a crush on someone who also likes me. I say this every day, don't I? It's true, and I'm going to be happy. I never thought I'd even consider the possibility that I could be this happy.

I wrote a draft of the letter I'll eventually send to my parents. That's how I'm going to tell them. I can't tell them in any other way. I guess I'm going to leave it up to them whether they want the rest of the family to find out. They can tell them if they want to.

January 5, 2006

You've got to think that there's something about not being able to show your love for someone that straight people just wouldn't get. The fear, I think, is not something that you can fully understand if you're straight and have never questioned it.

I imagine that, had I continued to keep to myself the fact that I'm gay, I would have become very bitter. There's something about the simple fact of isolation that makes people that way. But now I feel like I have somewhere to go – that there are people like me who get the way I think and behave, and who also face the same challenges that I do.

January 6, 2006

There's something about hearing a person have a phone conversation with their lover that definitely tells you more about them. The attitude they take – and there are three or four main ones – the "I'm the one who takes care of you," the "don't get mad; we'll do it your way," the "we're friends on equal footing," and the "c'mon – let's just love each other because anything else is a waste of time." You know what I mean?

January 7, 2006

That's my never-ending quest in life - to finally be where I feel like I belong. It's still on. I always think I've found that place, but then something happens to challenge that, and I must take action or become bitter and unhappy (I suppose those are one and the same).

This weekend is time to myself. I'm taking a lot of time to myself, actually. I need it. I need time, without the influence of others.

January 11, 2006

What do you say to someone who thinks they might be gay but is too afraid to admit to themselves that they do know? Nothing, really. There's nothing you can say, because people need to make their own connection with it in their own time.

January 12, 2006

I knew that I was gay for a pretty long time. I think I knew that I had to wait to come out, and that's why I kept telling myself that I wasn't sure. How long ago, I wonder, did I know? I remember as early as seventh or eighth grade – having crushes on girls and worrying that someone would get it.

I wonder if I could list them all; all the girls I had crushes on. There are many of them, so many that I'd probably miss a few. While I don't even think there were any guys. I never sought them out the way I did with girls.

I have to think that my mom at least has suspected – something. I guess I have a hard time believing that people haven't noticed my words and actions as they pertain to girls I've had crushes on. It's hard to believe because the feelings were always so strong inside of me that I feel it's almost impossible that I didn't give myself away. I almost wish that I had. Maybe I'll find out that I had.

I wonder if my being gay will influence my parents to think about their politics. Will they vote for the candidates that support equality for gay and straight people? Do they agree or disagree with the notion that gay people should be allowed to adopt children? I guess I would be disheartened if they didn't support either of those issues.

Then again, I can liken it to how I was treated as a child, and it's nothing new. Which is sad, but true. When has my father ever changed his thinking because of something I said – even when it was something that was hurting me?

I think that's the first time I've ever stated that calmly, as a fact. I feel like it's progress, and I feel like it'll all be okay, even if it's not.

I'm not going to perish. I'm a good person, and there are people around who are willing to help. I just get frustrated with not having anyone to talk very openly with. You get the feeling that most people would rather not. I think a big part is just that they don't understand it. The point of view is foreign to them.

January 13, 2006

I really want a girlfriend. Somebody to cuddle with, you know? The thought of cuddling with a girl excites me. I've never done it before. I imagine that it would be wonderful – especially if she feels the same way that I do.

Sometimes I think that what I'm looking for in terms of love isn't realistic. But then I think about how I've felt for people, and I think, if someone I feel about that way also feels the same, then that's it. That's what we search for. That intense feeling of wanting to do everything you can in order to be with someone and make them happy. In a healthy way, of course. Not in a weird obsessive way. And to know how to deal with it when that initial rush fades.

I just want to have a crush on someone, and now that I've admitted to myself that I'm gay, I don't want to have any more huge crushes on straight girls. I want to start having crushes on other lesbians.

What would it be like to meet someone and be attracted to her, and to know that I had a chance? Also, where do I stand on the lesbian scale? Am I cute? Where do I rank? Would I get hit on if I went to a bar or somewhere where there were a lot of lesbians? Where can I go to find lesbians? I have to find these things out. I'm pretty clueless, so far. It doesn't help that we keep a fairly low profile – on average. We're not as "out and about" as the gay boys. Wonder why that is.

January 14, 2006

Hung out with ▢▢▢ last night and fully expected to tell her that I'm gay. But it seems like every time I get face-to-face with a person, I chicken out.

I've told two people face-to-face. One more over the phone, and one more in writing. I think maybe I'll use the writing approach for a few more. I am for my parents, anyway.

I feel like coming out to my parents will, in some strange way, free me. I feel like it'll show them that I'm this unique person who has sides that they don't even know. Sides that are good – that express who I am and how I feel, and who could have thrived as such, had they seen and nurtured the good in me.

I'm sure they always saw good in me. They just never showed that they did, so how was I supposed to know? And how was I supposed to learn how to recognize it and nurture it in myself and others?

I'm learning, though. Somehow. It's a challenge, every day, to figure out what limitations I'm putting on myself, and what obstacles are within instead of external, as they appear to be. I have so much fear.

Fear of everything. But learning to overcome it.

(In Hindsight)

HOW THE INBOX
MADE OUTING EASIER

I came out via e-mail.

The first person I ever told, I told in an e-mail. Initially, most people I told got the news in an e-mail. I did tell a few people face-to-face, but those you can count on the fingers of one hand, and probably still have a couple left for other things. (What?)

To each of my parents I sent a package containing a letter, a book that I thought might answer a few questions, and an uplifting lesbian romantic comedy which was thoughtfully chosen from the myriad.

Let me tell you why I am an advocate of the electronic mail:

1. You can organize and say exactly what you want to say.

2. You can save it and come back to it later.

3. You can CC the world.

4. You're not there when they get the news.

5. You can deal with the responses when you want to.

Bottom line: It gives you a lot more control than you might have in a conversation.

I did worry that I was being a wuss about it and taking the easy way out. (And I can honestly say - that pun was completely unintentional.) But you know what? Coming out is coming out.

Does it still take courage to click "Send"? Hell, yes – it does.

Does it give you any more insight into how the other person will react and what aspects of your relationship might change? Not at all.

Who is the one putting herself out there, displaying vulnerability? You are.

Do it the way you want to do it.

For me, it went over a lot easier than expected. I have been lucky, and I hope I feel the same when I finally have a girlfriend to introduce.

January 15, 2006

I might like to move to West Hollywood. I think I'd enjoy transplanting myself into a culture that I've always belonged to without even knowing or fully being aware of it. I'd love to be able to walk into a public place and think that there's a possibility that someone might think I'm attractive whom I might also find attractive.

I want to flirt with someone, and think there's the chance it might end in a kiss. It's a foreign idea to me; something that's never happened with someone I really wanted to kiss.

All I know is what it's like to try to forget about feelings. To reconcile how something that feels so good can be so bad or unaccepted.

January 17, 2006

It's strange to live your life feeling like nobody really knows you, who you are, or why you are.

I've come to the conclusion that what we're really all trying to be, if you remove the things that handicap us, and our prejudices, is the same. And we really all are the same, but it's sometimes not in our best interests to be. I mean, for the sake of self-preservation and because of outside influences, sometimes we just can't. But we can hope to, someday.

All I know is that I'm working, every day, to make my life the best place it can be for me. It's a long, slow process. It involves finding courage and taking action even if I don't particularly want to. Well, I guess I sort of want to, or I wouldn't be doing it. But I think you know what I mean.

January 18, 2006

Sometimes when I wake up in the morning, I feel an emptiness inside. I don't know why. I find myself grasping for something to think about to fill the void, and it doesn't always work. Why, I wonder, do I also have this feeling in moments throughout any given day? Is this something that everyone goes through?

I tend to think that the answer is "yes." I think there are a lot of people in this world who pretend to be fine when they're not. And we have to, to some extent, to fit in with society and have friends – but we can also have honesty at the same time – honesty with ourselves and with one another.

That's one of my current challenges. I'm trying to be honest with people. I think I'm fairly honest with myself – except occasionally when I need to step up and take a responsible action for something only I can do, yet I don't want to do it. That's when I need to tell myself, "Tough. So what?" Getting better at it, though. Definitely speaking more of what's on my mind.

And in turn, trying to be there for others. Learning how to listen in a more empathetic way. I have lots to offer to the people around me, I think.

It helped to acknowledge that I'm gay, because I feel like I finally found who I've always been – and now the challenge is to create my world so that I'm comfortable being who I've always been. Takes some time when you're so entrenched in your life and set in your relationships with people.

January 19, 2006

I feel utterly exposed. I came out to two people, yesterday. I'm getting better at this. The wonderful thing is that once it's out there, it's out there. There's no taking it back, and I'm forced to commit fully, to keep talking, which is a very new experience for me. I'm not usually apt to commit to things that expose me like that.

It's sort of like acting, I'd imagine. Which is ironic, because for the first time, I'm not acting.

I need to acknowledge that everyone else's thought process isn't what I predicted it to be, so I can't assume that everyone knows anything.

Talking about it is going to be useful to me. I feel like I can speak about something that I know. And these are things that come from the truest part of me. That place has always been there; it's just been hard to access because when you shut off one part, it's difficult to know what you should or can let through. I surprise myself every day.

I guess I'm writing an e-mail to my friends. I just need to put aside my fears about people interpreting things from the past in this new light. I can't do anything about it. I have to admit that that part is completely out of my control, and it can't be avoided if I'm going to tell them.

It sucks that people will still be surprised after knowing me for 10+ years. I guess that gives them an interesting life experience, too. The first time a good friend comes out to you. What can you do? Nothing different, or you shouldn't, anyway.

January 20, 2006

Last night, I wrote an e-mail in which I came out to my friends from high school. I haven't read the two replies I got.

I guess the bottom line is that I'm much better at hiding things than I thought I was. Who knows, though. Maybe all the people I lived with in college do or did suspect.

Maybe I was more obvious to live with. I don't know.

I still just wish that I had some lesbian friends. I want, for the first time in my life, to be friends with people like me. I think that's going to be a revelation. I mean, I'm almost 24 years old, and I don't know what that's like.

January 22, 2006

Sometimes I think that I don't have a creative bone left in my body. It feels that way.

Sometimes, I try to remember how it was before, and I have a difficult time. I can't. I don't want to go back to those feelings, though. Of feeling so dark inside, like there was never going to be anything that could make me happy that I'd be lucky enough to have.

I always had a fire inside, though. Contradictory. The hopelessness and the fire would war against each other so that it would turn into resentment.

I don't like being resentful. When I find myself that way, I need to remind myself to choose one – the hopelessness or the fire. And I know better than to choose hopelessness. It's not what got me here.

January 23, 2006

Why do I feel like things need to be done all at once, in one big flurry of activity? Why can't I keep a steady pace and move forward in increments? "Obsessive personality" is what I call it. It's like I need to get it done all at once – and quickly – because I'll lose the opportunity if it takes too long, as if whomever's attention I had for a moment will suddenly be gone if I take too long.

I can see this happening. I'm sure it has happened – with my mom; with my dad. They never got how important it was for me to feel like something I did made them happy. And by the time they expressed any of it, I'd built a defense against it. I'm more afraid of positive emotions from them than I am of negative ones. Funny how it works, but it's absolutely true.

I wish things were easier. I wish…that people didn't judge so easily. I wish that people weren't discriminated against because of who they love. Don't you think that's a horrible basis for discrimination?

Everyone focuses on the sex part, but it's really not about the sex. I mean, you want to have sex, but when you're in love, the sex is secondary to the emotions. Sex is simply an expression of those emotions, which exist separately.

I want to feel those things, and I want to physically express those feelings. It's odd, being almost 24 and not having been in a relationship with anyone that I really wanted to be with. I feel completely new.

I had this thought today, that to figure out what fits, you should imagine yourself driving down a highway through the desert, at 2 a.m. Who's sleeping in the passenger seat next to you? It's such an intimate thing that it says a lot about you.

IN)SANITY LETTERS: PART III

EVERYWHERE

I see romance everywhere. I think that the world is romantic, and the romance I see is not limited to the love between two people. It's between what exists and what the human spirit wants to exist. It's the game we play with the universe; the chance that opens us to the possibilities that life is so much more than we ever thought it could be. That's romantic.

I see romance everywhere, and I'll show you. Everything has a soul, a story – if you just have the patience to see it. All connected, and I want you with me to experience it – to recognize that what we live is beautiful.

The sky, covered in specks of stardust when the earth's filter is below and behind – an awesome sight; one that makes you feel as if you never mattered in the history of existence, but also as if you were always a part of it – maybe you are a tiny speck against the backdrop of the universe, only knowing what you can know; only knowing that we are here now and nothing else matters.

'I love you,' I think in this moment, and I'm not even sure if I've spoken it to you, the universe, or myself. Isn't it all the same? Can't be - because as your lips touch mine, I feel the warmth of connection – although it could be that this is the culmination of an inevitable reunion – that we are the same, and the same as the universe – two pieces of it coming back together, not knowing from where it was we came, but somehow feeling that we must now touch and realize we can never be apart.

I see romance everywhere. Come with me, and you'll see. I can turn anything into a story of triumph. My life and yours. I like to believe that everything was deliberate. Not our actions, but the actions of the universe; its energy. A natural order that pulls things together; people to people and the result is what we experience as life.

I wonder why we were pulled together – you and I. What's our end?

January 24, 2006

Am I growing up too quickly, or too slowly? I don't know. It sometimes seems too quick, but too slow because I'm missing a lot of the things that one is supposed to pick up over the natural course of development.

It's scary, and I wonder what other people see. I worry too much about what other people think. I wonder if they humor me, or if my thoughts are founded in reality. I think I have a pretty good grasp of the way things really are, but trying to confirm that fact is something that just tends to make me feel like I'm going crazy.

And I realize, over and over again, that the only one I can really count on is myself. There are things that I can't let others do for me, and I also can't run away from. Those are the things in which I just need to listen to whatever it is inside of me that's telling me where to go, and just go there.

Everything happens in its own time, I think, and as long as I work on living my life as I want to live it, and honorably, I don't think there's anything to regret.

I'm working on being more comfortable with things and people, and there's a part of me that wants to hope that I get the results I want, and I will hope, but I also know that sometimes things don't work out exactly that way. I can't lose confidence in myself, and I can't think that I'm going to spend the rest of my years doing something that doesn't fulfill me.

I still want to make a difference in the world. I want to affect people – to cause them to think and change their lives in a positive way.

January 25, 2006

Is this normal? Is it normal for one to feel terrified of life? Well, not life, I guess, but of the future? Of not having everything that one wants to have? That sounds weird. Of not being happy?

But happiness is a choice, isn't it? I thought it was. And I always wonder – how much of something is my problem? I'm entitled to my feelings, right, but where's the line between where I should try to change things and where I should just deal with it and accept it as something that's just going to happen? I guess I don't really have such a great sense for that kind of thing because of the way I grew up.

I feel like coming out to my parents would be a sort of pivotal turning point in my life; a moment where I declare to be my own person, and not just who they think I am, or who they tell me I am. That's all I've been to them, and every time there's something uniquely me, it gets pushed on the side.

It's difficult to hold on to those things; to know as a child that you need to protect those parts of yourself because the ones who are supposed to be taking care of you are the ones who endanger it the most. It's not a good feeling. That's where you begin to not trust those you've been forced to depend on – the people that you should have trust in, if you have trust in anyone. But when you're being endangered like that, and you realize why that is, you know what you have to do – stop trusting and start depending on yourself.

As a kid, it's a horrible thing to do. I did it. And I wish sometimes that I could go back and know all the things that had to have happened in order to make me this person I am today, but it's impossible. I can't remember, and I can't go back. Lost forever are the moments in which my heart must have been broken enough for me to stop letting others help me to put it back together.

Children shouldn't have to live through things like that. There are kids who live through worse, I know. If I could take away their pain, I would.

January 20, 2006

This is fun. Who ever would have thought I'd feel that way about coming out and being out?

On *The L Word*, in the first season, Dana wasn't yet out, but her friends kept telling her that she was "really, really gay." Or "so gay."

I feel that way about myself – that I'm very, very gay. And I can't keep letting it not make the surface. I can't keep censoring myself. I have had so many crushes on so many girls. I feel so gay.

I wonder if that's something that each individual person feels differently about. I actually love how gay I am. Now that I've accepted it for myself. There are all of these things about me that I'm not going to try to change, because I can't. And maybe because of that, or maybe because I'm me, I don't want to. Change it, that is. I just want to be and to do.

January 31, 2006

I sent the packages to my parents. THE packages. One for each, because it would be complicated to make them share.

I met up with my co-worker +●◊●+ and her girlfriend and one of their friends for dinner and a movie tonight. My first social engagement with out lesbians. And I felt empowered. I was excited. Well, maybe a little nervous, but not anxious.

I have confidence. I have so much more confidence as a lesbian, because that's who I actually am. You know? I mean, it's no wonder why I didn't have any confidence being who I wasn't.

I had always thought that I was supposed to be a certain way, and that I was inadequate because of all these things that didn't (and don't) come naturally to me. It really is amazing.

So anyway, on the drive home, I felt so proud and sure that I could be as happy as I wanted to be, regardless of what my parents thought, and I resolved to send the packages, even though I'd been waiting for the ideal time. So I drove all the way to the Westchester/LAX post office at 9:30 pm, and just dumped the packages into the mail bin.

I was talking on the phone with ●◊+◊● at the time, which was good because she kept me from doing too much thinking about my actions – about sending the packages, and before I knew it, I had dropped them in the mail drop, and I knew I could no longer do anything. Couldn't get it back.

February 1, 2006

I realized last night that my best-case scenario would be for my parents to say that they already knew. My worst case scenario would be that they were completely surprised and that they'd start trying to show their love for me. That would take some getting used to.

February 2, 2006

There are now a few other lesbians at work. It was like I started coming out, and the universe made sure I had the necessary people around to support me and help me to continue my growth.

◊●◊●◊ made it okay for me. She made me okay with it.

I feel like it's just going to be weird in general – dating girls. I want to. That's what's so weird. To be excited about dating. To want to date. I've never had that experience before.

It's so intense – I think about how strongly I've felt for some of the girls I've fallen for, and I can't even imagine what it would be like to feel that way about someone and be able to kiss her and do all the things I've fantasized about doing with her.

After a lifetime of acting like you can't have what you want, it gets a little scary to start thinking that maybe you *can* have what you want. And then you get excited about it, but you still can't even imagine what it would be like and you think it would feel so right, but you've never had that sense of "rightness" before, so you can't really imagine that, either.

I can't wait to see what I'm like in a relationship. I think I would be an extremely loving and caring girlfriend. I think I'm a pretty good catch, actually. I'm reasonably cute, smart, funny, and employed.

February 3, 2006

Going to see *Imagine Me & You* tonight, which is a lesbian romantic comedy.

I can't seem to say the word "lesbian" enough. It's like I want to talk about it all the time, which I guess is only natural, given that I spent my whole life not talking about it.

We grow up being told that these things that we want that feel so natural and good are wrong, and that we should want something entirely different – what everybody else seems to want.

Some people struggle to be different, but I've never had to make an effort at that. For me, it's a struggle to fit in. It doesn't really matter in what sense.

Each of us has an inner truth – a truth to which we must be loyal, or die whether physically or figuratively. I used to have to push back, in order to protect that truth. But it's okay. I'm working on getting out there, and I'm working on dealing with things. Learning to live, in the world – and to thrive in it.

I'm happy, but I'd like to be happier. Ha. I don't know what kind of a statement that is. The world is overwhelming, and really, the best way, the most effective way to make a difference, is to look at what's right in front of you. Change that, and you change your world. And really, when it comes down to it, how is your world separate from anybody else's?

February 5, 2006

I so need to be with someone right now who will support me while I listen to my voicemail and read the e-mail from my parents. I can't do this alone, which is very weird. I've never felt as if I couldn't do it – anything – alone. Except for this.

This is such a gut-wrenching process – not because I'm afraid of how they're going to react, but because I'm opening myself up. The vulnerability is killing me. This is, hands down, the most difficult emotional thing that I've ever had to do.

I keep trying to think of someone who I'd be comfortable going to with this, who would just take care of me. I just want someone to sit next to me, take the phone from my hands, and play the message. And click through my e-mail and just read it for me.

I can't make myself do it right now. And I can't hang out with anyone who doesn't know, right now.

Soon, everyone will know, because I'm too tired of being a muted version of myself. I'm too tired of continuing to suppress the things I want to do and say.

I can't believe that my parents know. My parents know that I'm gay. I told them that I'm gay. I'm a little bit paralyzed.

(In Hindsight)

TO BE <u>LIKE</u> HER, OR TO BE <u>FOR</u> HER... ...THAT IS THE QUESTION.

I knew that I wanted, in some way, to mention the people who helped me to take the leaps I have taken in my life.

But I sat down to write it, and I had about five false starts. I was blocked. Usually when I'm blocked, it means either that I'm lying to myself, or that I'm trying to generalize a specific situation into an all-encompassing anecdote that doesn't quite work.

I thought about this, and I realized that I was doing both. And usually when I do that, it's because I think that speaking specifically will reveal too much. In other words, I'm afraid to share. When I stopped lying to myself, it wasn't hard to see why.

The people who have helped me the most are wonderful people in their own right - they are unique and strong and compassionate and wise and funny and exactly the kind of people that I hope to find someday in one special person.

And they are all women.

It wouldn't be inaccurate to say that maybe, in some cases, they didn't do anything specific to help me. I helped myself because I wanted to be worthy of them. It gave me courage to commit to doing things that I probably never would have, had the reason been simply that it was good for me.

Had I written this in the self-deception that was my first impulse, I would have claimed hero worship - admiration and the desire to walk in great footsteps. Instead, although the heroines and their footsteps are no less, I will attribute it to whatever it is that makes each of us, despite a lifetime of fears and flaws, give everything she is - to be, for another human being, a better person.

February 7, 2006

So I actually checked my voicemails and e-mail last night. I'm relieved because my parents acted in a way that I know how to handle – they don't really care that I'm gay; I mean that it doesn't matter to them. But then it was suddenly all about them again, and the ways in which I don't live up to their expectations or don't behave the way they want me to behave. I know how to deal with that – keep acting the way I've always acted with them.

February 10, 2006

Went to my first girl bar, tonight. Interesting, fun. It's going to be tough to find a girlfriend because lesbians are homebodies. I'm a homebody, and I like it, but that just makes it a little difficult for lesbians to find each other.

February 19, 2006

There was a sex scene on *The L Word* that totally turned me on. I'm not used to letting myself be okay with that kind of stuff. But it's awesome. It's amazing, actually. I think girls are hot. I think girls are sexy. I get turned on by girls that I think are hot and sexy. I really, really want to kiss a girl. I want to be intimate with a girl, emotionally and physically. I want to fall in love with a girl.

February 20, 2006

How wonderful it is to be able to tell myself and the people around me that I'm attracted to a girl. I mean, really. To know that what I'm feeling is sexual attraction and to allow myself to feel it and feel okay about it and maybe even nurture it… It's like nothing I've ever experienced before in my life. Something I never really knew existed, I guess.

It still amazes me how people who are different have to figure out what it is that doesn't line up with what everyone else tells them they should be experiencing. It's a lot of pain and struggle and inner conflict and contradiction, but when you know who you are and what you're feeling and what you want, finally, it must feel 10 times better than it would if you had grown up knowing and understanding and conscious of it all along.

Does that even make sense? In a way, I think it does – because everything is relative and it depends on the range – a person's frame of reference. The wider your frame of reference, the more you can experience, I think. I'm grateful for all my experiences. I wouldn't be where I am without them. Still, I think that life is definitely just more difficult for some people – and for me, I've turned it into a thing that motivates me.

My life… the struggle is what makes it great. The struggle is why I'm going to end up where I'm going to end up. I have something to share with the world, and I sometimes worry that I don't really. I worry that I have delusions of grandiosity. But if they help me to actually achieve things, then I guess they weren't so much delusions, after all.

February 26, 2006

It's impossible, I think, to be fully conscious of everything about ourselves. It would be some very strange form of insanity, I think, but I also believe that some people are just more willing to go there than others are. Some are deathly afraid and don't want to know, while others crave it; need it, in order to convince themselves that there is hope to make different what things we acknowledge.

I'm of the latter. I need to acknowledge things. It's important to me that a situation be addressed as what it truly is, and that anyone being disrespected should be acknowledged, as well.

Sometimes, I don't stand up for myself, and I'm working on that. I've become a lot better at it, lately. I just… I know what I want, and I know a lot better who I am, although I don't know if we ever really know fully who we are until we're faced with tough decisions and circumstances and situations. It's not like I haven't been, but I also think that we change. Our decision process matures, and it becomes part of us – and living through the consequences changes us, too.

February 27, 2006

I'd like to get back to being an artist. I think I still kind of am, in my everyday life, and somehow I just seem to always not quite fit in, which I think automatically makes one an artist in what one must go through to relate to other people.

What Heather Matarazzo said about gay people having a hard time relating to others before they're quite sure of who and what they are, struck me as true in my own experience. It was more difficult to relate to people, but now that I know where the difference comes from – or what it is – it's somehow easier to feel like I empathize with others. Sometimes there's a necessary translation, as there will always be in a world of heterosexuals, but it's so much easier.

People say that we're living in enlightened times – that society has accepted differences in sexual orientation, and I get the feeling that we're supposed to be happy and content with that – because it's better than it was before. That's logical, but it still doesn't make sense. I can't get married. I can't adopt a child with my partner. Young people still commit suicide over it.

That's perhaps the great tragedy. I don't need to get married. I don't need to adopt a child. But what is the world missing out on when a teenager takes his or her own life because what's supposed to be the greatest thing about human existence is instead a source of only pain and anguish?

People who are different are the ones who affect change – they're the ones who make things better – maybe because they don't think about losing. Maybe you have to pretend that failure doesn't exist and take success for granted. Is that how I got here? In some ways, I think it is. And I'll keep doing it.

March 6, 2006

I guess I never thought about this – when you're gay, you don't take honesty for granted. You don't take for granted the gift of being free to be yourself. That makes you conscious of a lot of things. Whereas, if you're straight and have never doubted it, you've never really had a reason to think about all these things. And that's not bad. It just means you've never had to deal with it.

It's such a revelation – being able to look and watch and think, "that's hot" or "she's pretty." And then I'm realizing that there are some girls who I'll always be attracted to – who I would go for in an instant if they expressed an interest in me. Those are the ones I need to be careful around. They'll know now that I'm flirting with them, which isn't all bad. I like flirting. And if they like flirting with me, then who gets hurt? Nobody, unless I fall in love.

IN)SANITY LETTERS: PART IV

STAY

You still make me feel like the world is ending when you walk away. Small worlds end and I wonder if I'll ever lose hope.

CRUSHES

*You know how it is when you wished for
something that didn't happen,*

and it might have been a long time ago,

but you don't want anyone to know

*because you're afraid of the vulnerability
that comes with expressing
what you wanted?*

There are still some stories I won't tell.

March 10, 2006

I feel like I've hit a wall with coming out. I still have all of my friends from school to tell. I think it's been maybe a month since I told my parents. I need to keep taking more steps.

March 13, 2006

I just wrote a whole bunch more "I'm gay" e-mails. By tomorrow night, they'll all know. How fucking scary.

Why is coming out so damn difficult? I'm so much more out now than I have ever been, and I still imagine a freer environment in which to flourish. I feel like by being completely open with everyone and everything, I'm clearing the way for the synchronicity of the universe to present me with what I want. It couldn't hurt.

I'm proud of myself. I'm proud of myself and thankful to everyone. So far, everyone has been great. I was so prepared to lose friends. And who knows - maybe someday I will. But right now, I'm very satisfied with the responses I've gotten from people.

Ultimately, I want to be able to talk about the things that straight people take for granted - the freedom to say out loud, in a public place, who they think is sexy.

March 14, 2006

I'm a little scared to check my e-mail today. Ripping myself open takes energy and effort, both of which are exhausting when combined with anticipation. Anticipation is just exhausting, I think.

March 15, 2006

I still haven't checked my e-mail from yesterday. There's a pattern here. I muster the courage to write and send the e-mail, but then I'm afraid to read the responses - or rather, I avoid reading the responses - because that gives me the feeling of being utterly exposed. Somehow, that's more intimate than writing the e-mails.

The funny part is that I'm not even worried about what people will say. Just having the dialogue is an intimacy that freaks me out. It's occurred to me that maybe it means I'm not ready? But I don't think I can put that on myself. I can do it in whatever marginal way I choose to do it, and I'll still have done it. It's probably less uncomfortable for the people I'm telling, as well.

Really, though, I'm so proud of myself. I never thought I'd be doing this, and now that I am, other things are so much easier, too. I just feel less afraid because after this, pretty much everything else is lesser.

To accept that I am gay and to tell everyone in my life - that's something that just sort of spits in the face of the fear and anxiety I've had for all of my life. I feel like my life before this was controlled by that fear - or determined by that fear - and now, that's no longer the case.

I've done what I was so afraid of doing. Which means that I can do other things that I'm afraid of doing. Rejection is outside of myself. Rejection doesn't change who I am or my convictions. And I don't have control over other people. All I have control over are my actions.

I had an interesting reaction on the phone with my grandma, last night. She brought up the letter and said that everything is still the same; she loves me just the same as before; she wants me to be happy. And I got defensive. I said something along the lines of, "I know - I mean, I don't need anybody's approval."

And I instantly felt bad. But there were two emotions battling, and given that, anger will always win its way to expression - for me, anyway. So there was anger - at the fact that people think they have the power to make me feel good about it by telling me that it's okay. Then there was relief that everything would still be the same. Interesting how, given the choice, even unconsciously, I will express anger over any emotion that makes me feel vulnerable.

March 16, 2006

I guess I have major vulnerability issues. I never really looked at it before. I always thought - intimacy or receiving attention/love was the problem, but really, it's being vulnerable that causes a lot of my resistance with people.

I think that's a breakthrough discovery, because I never looked at it as something that was not existing. Does that make sense? Like if you picture me, and someone I'm close to, if you picture the obstacle in between us, the thing keeping us apart, it was always something floating in the air, blocking. Something that was malleable, that could be shaped and sculpted and bent into whatever I had to shape it into.

But realizing that a lot of the problem is vulnerability makes me picture nothing between me and the other person; nothing blocking, and that makes me feel nervous and afraid and insecure.

I need to realize that vulnerability is necessary for a happy, intimate relationship. With that comes risk. And that's what you're taking a chance on when you trust people.

Vulnerability isn't only necessary for me revealing my life to people; it's also necessary in my being an empathetic and comforting presence when other people are revealing things about their lives. It's just necessary, period. And that's what I need to work on.

Fascinating. I'd never thought about it that way.

There's also a line between healthy vulnerability and being a drama queen, and that's not one I'd want to overstep.

March 29, 2006

I like the way attraction feels. I like finding myself smiling at a daydream of someone. It just feels good. I hope that I find someone soon who I can flirt with, and who flirts back and wants to kiss me and be with me as much as I do her.

March 31, 2006

Now that I've accepted who I'd love, I have an entirely different experience when listening to love songs and watching romantic movies. Now I can take them for what they are without getting angry and bitter and resentful and rejecting them.

Specifically, I heard Garth Brooks's "She's Every Woman" on the radio a few minutes ago, and I got all warm and fuzzy and mushy because that's how I want to feel about the girl I fall in love with.

That's probably just the feeling of being in love. You probably can't avoid it.

It frustrates me that I now know very clearly how to recognize my feelings of attraction, and yet there's no one to act on them with.

I keep wondering if I'm cute. I have no clue. What if I'm not as desired as it takes in order to be approached by someone at a bar or something? What if all the lesbians think I'm straight? No, I know that probably wouldn't happen. But still - what if somehow, lesbians aren't attracted to me?

AGE 24

I always think I've found the girl of my dreams, except that she's usually straight and if she's not, I'm just too short.

April 2, 2006

I feel like I'm part of a community. Feels so good to know that there are things I do that show that I belong to this group of people - that I fit in because I am who I am. It's all I've ever wanted - to fit in with a group of people because I'm like them, and to have them appreciate me because I'm myself, but also because I'm like them. Does that make sense? It does to me. And it feels good.

April 7, 2006

I cringe when I think about going back to look at some of my writing. It was so infused with emotion - with my wanting to get something out there that was very difficult to say and to come to terms with.

I had a hard time coming to terms with the fact that I was gay. I was so afraid. If I can share that with other girls who are going through the same thing, and make it a bit easier for them - because I went through all of this alone. I went through it never having talked to anyone about it, not having had any actual lesbian encounters.

I'm only now at a point where I realize that I'm not hiding anything. I'm not keeping anything hidden inside. I'm still getting over it - dealing with the loss of the bitterness and anger and resentment that I held inside for so long.

Letting go of that is scary because I'm left open for good feelings. It takes away the wall and leaves space. Just space. And it's up to me.

April 8, 2006

I don't know when I actually knew that I was gay. I always thought about it as a possibility. Actually, I noticed at a very young age, probably before I even knew what "gay" was, that I had some feelings toward girls and women that I sensed were somehow different in a way that wasn't to be expressed or talked about.

I don't remember when I learned what "gay" was. The feelings I had are so clear to me now, but I think I was in denial for a painfully long time.

And now... I just feel like, "Thank God." You know? I mean, thank God (in the figurative sense) that I made the decision to be honest with myself and with everyone else. It felt awkward at first, but I'm getting used to it, and when I think about it, I'm so proud and so happy.

April 10, 2006

I feel like I'm being watched. Okay, maybe not so much "watched" as "being kept an eye on."

At this point, everyone knows that I've never had sex - at all - or even kissed a girl. They all, especially the people older than me, are waiting on the edges of their seats. They want to see. I mean, not *see*, but - see. My reaction.

They just want me to be happy, because I think they know about being out there and trying to find someone - gay or straight - and they just want me to fall in love.

I've been in love, but never with anyone who I thought would ever love me back. I became good at hiding things, holding back. Part of me is afraid of the intensity of my feelings. I've always held back. I'm not sure what would happen if I didn't.

April 14, 2006

The thrill of coming out is finally wearing off, and I'm settling in to reality, which is this - I'm not going to meet anyone if I'm working all the time or sitting alone in my apartment.

April 16, 2006

Do you think that maybe the gay community as a whole is less tolerant of bullshit than the other part of American society? Do you think that's what comes about when the basic instinct "to be" is a constant struggle, a fight against bullshit? When it's intrinsic like that? And maybe we're less afraid for having been forced to take on the responsibility to fight for survival.

April 20, 2006

I think I've run out of people to tell that I'm gay. Never thought I'd find myself here. It's kind of anti-climactic. Is there such a thing as post-coming-out depression? Kind of like post-partum depression, but without the baby. I'll bet that other people go through this, too. It seems a natural thing to happen when you haven't dated anyone, ever. What do people do?

April 24, 2006

Friday night. Went to a bar with some friends, one of whom I hadn't seen in awhile. She knows how to party, and she'd found out that day that I had come out.

She's not gay, but I had her attention the entire night, most of it spent on the dance floor. Nothing huge happened, but it was good.

There were moments when I felt like everything was absolutely right, you know? It wasn't about her; it was about what and who she represented.

At one point, she grabbed my hand and led me to the bathroom. And I just followed, and I thought, this is so what I'm supposed to be doing. I'm so supposed to be with a girl. There was chemistry between us, and it wasn't that it was her, specifically, it was that I was with a sexy girl, and she felt good to me, and I liked where I felt I was with her.

Does that make any sense? I'm trying to articulate this for myself... It's like, with guys, I always feel awkward because I'm not "the girl." I'm not a girly girl, but it's not even like that. It's like there's no place for me to be with a guy that just feels right. There's no chemistry. I think that's what it is. Things don't just fall into place - I don't fall into a place where I feel comfortable.

But with a girl, it's like stuff just clicks. I know where I am. And while on the level of a relationship with a guy, I'm always aware that something's out-of-whack, that he's a guy and I'm a girl and it's supposed to work but it isn't... With a girl, I'm not aware of that. I cease to be conscious of what she is and what I am. I become nothing but me. And it's not a conscious effort.

When I'm with a girl, I'm only conscious of the fact that I'm a girl in the sense that it feels so damn good. Otherwise, I'm just me. It fits.

And on that dance floor, what felt so good was that in that moment, I was more "me" than I have ever been. And maybe all the crushes I've ever had, all these girls I've fallen in love with... Maybe what kept me there, liking them, was the fact that when I felt what I felt, I felt me. And maybe that's why I sort of looked at everybody else on the dance floor that night, and I thought – fuck 'em.

May 21, 2006

I picked up a book of lesbian coming out stories at the bookstore today – I mean, I picked it up and held it in my hands; not that I bought it. I felt the urge – well, not the urge – the desire – to read it, to experience what it might be like to read the experiences and stories of others I might be able to relate to in that way – but something held me back.

I wanted to know peoples' stories and to relate, but I was afraid to go through the experience of reading the stories – of experiencing the way one does when one reads a story – to feel the feelings of the characters as one's own. It's what I love about fiction, and what scared me about these particular stories. I guess that'll have to wait.

June 11, 2006

I went with +●◊●+ and a few of her friends to the Annual Gay Pride event in West Hollywood. I'd never experienced anything like the Pride Parade. I can't express how wonderful it felt to be part of something that I knew I belonged in - to know that there are a lot of us who feel the same way about certain things, and that despite being treated the way we are by society, culture, and the law, we are still here, speaking out, trying to educate each other and to make positive changes for ourselves and for people in the future.

One of the groups marching in the parade was the Pop Luck Club, which are gay fathers and their children, whether biological or adopted, I'm guessing. So of course they also had children walking with them. One of +●◊●+'s friends jokingly said, "Wow, those kids have already figured out that they're gay? That's great!"

The kids were all no older than five, and they obviously were there because their fathers were gay, and it had no bearing on whether they, themselves, were gay, but his comment struck me and I got a little emotional.

It's obvious that "figuring it out" is a first rite of passage that every gay person goes through. Whether you're out or not, you know what that struggle is like. And it's not something that anyone who has gone through it will take lightly, because they know what it means.

Then when the part of the parade with schools and education and tolerance in the school system and curriculum came by, the cheers got louder and everyone - in my group at least, was standing and clapping, and I felt how much they meant it – that this was something real that we would probably go to great lengths to support – because we know. And what I felt, the underlying cause of the conviction, was experience and pain. But pain that had been overcome – overcome for each of us individually, but with the knowledge that it still goes on, that it still happens to other people every day, and that it needs to stop.

June 17, 2006

On Thursday, I did a strange thing and went out by myself. To a bar. Or was it a lounge? Or a club? I don't know. I think that most places are all three – except for clubs that are actually clubs.

I figured that as long as I'm with other people, I'm probably not going to attempt to speak to anyone else. So I knew I'd have to start going alone. I just didn't know if I actually would.

But on Thursday, I thought, maybe I'll go tonight. And then later that day, I thought, I don't know if I'll go tonight. But I guess I got ready, got in my car, drove to West Hollywood, parked (and the night could have ended there; if you've ever tried to park in WeHo, you know what I mean) – got into the club, ordered a drink, sat down and guzzled it, and thought, I don't know if I'll go tonight.

That's how physical the process was, but I'm learning that sometimes, if I wait for my brain to catch up to my actions, nothing gets fuckin' done. Evidenced by the fact that thus far, no fucking has been done. It's true.

Anyway, I sat there and I called a few friends because they wouldn't have believed I'd gone, otherwise. Then I hung up, sat and looked around and kept drinking, and then when the crowd finally began to form, went inside to be a wallflower. I thought that wall-flowering might lead to something else. It didn't for about 20 minutes.

Then a girl came up to me and asked me why I was there alone. I didn't know, so I said, "I don't know." She asked if I smoked; I said "No." She asked if I wanted to go outside and talk; I said "Yeah."

So we went out on the patio and I met her straight guy friend who was waiting for his straight guy friend whom he hadn't told that it was lesbian night. When he got there, we went back inside and she got me another drink which was definitely more potent than the first one I'd had.

The more I drank, the easier it was to dance, so we danced. I realized later that I actually danced less with her than I did with her guy friend who thought he was at a straight club. Whatever.

That's what we did for awhile, and then she got a phone call and they had to leave, but not before getting my number. Turns out she thought my name was Nancy, to which I took absolutely no offense because I didn't know her name at all.

They left, I walked around and then got in the bathroom line and realized that I need some practice at coordinating the length of time it takes to get into the bathroom at a club, with how badly I need to go. Luckily, everyone was dancing anyway.

I peed, did a few more circles around the place, and decided that I was done for the night. I left, walked back to my car, and realized that it would be awhile before I could drive. So I drunk-called a friend, sat in my car for about 45 minutes, and then went home.

So I've got a number and she has mine, but I'll probably not call her... didn't quite click.

June 18, 2006

I still haven't come out to my roommate. Maybe she already knows, but I can't tell. Isn't that backwards? That the roommate would be the last to know? I can't even get that part right.

June 22, 2006

I can't quite name what I feel inside. I'm caught in this exciting, wonderful place between who I have been and who I am becoming. It's like I don't know anything, but at the same time, I know myself better than I ever have before.

I'm still terrified, and it feels really good – like at least I know that I'm not static; I'm moving forward and taking great strides toward the life I want to have.

It takes discipline. I've found that courage and bravery don't matter as much as discipline. I have come to believe that if you have discipline in the appropriate things, you can do anything.

July 12, 2006

I still use pronouns cautiously. Maybe not cautiously, but self-consciously. "They" and "them" instead of "she" and "her." Or "someone" instead of "a girl." I'd like to stop doing that.

It's weird how revealing your choice of pronoun can be. Like I express everything I feel about someone, just by using the word "she" - "she is," "she does," "she says," ...it feels intimate. I like it.

July 15, 2006

Last night, I went on my first date with a girl. We met online, and I didn't think it was a date at the time, but she said it was. And I didn't mind. It was fun.

I'm so scared, I think just because this is new. I've never been here before. I've never been in a situation where there was a clear and unobstructed path to a romantic relationship – emotionally. I never had to make the decision to let someone be close to me in that way.

And you know what – I might still be hung up on one of my recent crushes, and ++++ (my date) is self-admittedly still hung up on her ex-girlfriend. So maybe this is just a date-for-the-sake-of-dating thing for both of us.

July 17, 2006

Met with ++++ again after work today. I don't think she's my type. She has a lot of good qualities, but I don't think she's my type.

I hate this. I really do.

I can keep wishing,
but I'd better keep fishing,
'cause an imagined fish
in an empty boat
does not a dinner make.

Unblock, unlock the gates.

Beyond, it drops straight down – did you think there was a road? Ruts or tracks that you could follow, in a convoy or a caravan – a train? No. It drops straight down, to where you can't see.

What happened to everyone before? Can you ever know? Each falls her own, and even if two jumped at once, the winds would take them far from. An updraft, a vacuum – so that coming back together again is either by chance, or by choice. And just as likely as never again.

What happens on the way down? Your stomach catches in your throat and you can tense up, shut down, think of your death. Or you can force yourself into the moment, into each microsecond like a captured still from the whole motion of your fall, and in the stillness, unfreeze, break it, spread your arms and catch with your heart the next wave. Ride it. Ride it and try not to think. Thinking turns you inward, and you need to be out there – feeling.

You might never come down, and you don't need to. And someday, who knows when, you can look down and see that you are passing once again the gates through which you fell...

How did you get up so high?

myspace.com/figuringitoutbook

figuringitoutbook@gmail.com